YOUTH IN THE CITY

YOUTH IN THE CITY

The Church's Response to the Challenge of Youth Work

Peter Stow
with
Mike Fearon

HODDER AND STOUGHTON
LONDON SYDNEY AUCKLAND TORONTO

British Library Cataloguing in Publication Data

Stow, Peter
  Youth in the city : the Church's response
  to the challenge of youth work. —
  (Hodder Christian paperbacks).
  1. Church work with youth — Great Britain
  I. Title   II. Fearon, Mike
  259'.2'0941   BV4447

ISBN 0 340 41047 7

*Hodder & Stoughton Editorial Office: 47 Bedford Square, London WC1B
3DP.*

Contents

Acknowledgments   7
Foreword by Christopher Idle   9

PART ONE

1 Wastage   13
2 A Day at a Time   22
3 Open Youth Work   32
4 Youth Evangelism   45
5 Training   57
6 Detached Youth Work   67
7 The Pressures   78
8 Programme and Expansion   90

PART TWO

9   Education and Home Environment   105
10 Homelessness and Unemployment   118
11 Violence and Crime   132
12 Drink and Drugs   146
13 Racism and Sexism   156
14 Sex and Morality   168
15 Church in the City   180
16 Young Blood in the Church   191

Bibliography   203

Acknowledgments

We are grateful for the assistance given to us in the preparation of this book by the librarians at the British Library reading room, and at the London Institute For Contemporary Christianity. Our basic bibliographic source was the Youth section in the British Library, subject index 1975-85, though other material not listed there was also consulted. Our own selected list of the best of this material is featured at the end of this book. We extend our gratitude to all the authors listed there, for the groundwork which made our own task so much easier.

Most of the material in this book, however, derives from Pete's own life and work experience. We are indebted to Pete's friends and colleagues, who contributed so freely to the many hours of taped discussion which has added so much to the scope and depth of the book; particularly to Nick, Vernon, Phil, Karl, Peter, Sue, Kevin and Steve. Special thanks go to John Pearce for his help and encouragement – and for his constant bantering with Pete, to get his invaluable experiences and knowledge down in book form!

We received much help from the members of St Paul's club, whose stories and experiences are related herein. Their names have been changed in order to protect their anonymity. We are grateful too, to the East End clergy who were interviewed by me originally for an article in *Today* magazine. Much of that material is repeated here, in order that its use may continue. Other material has previously appeared in *Strait* and *Christian Family* magazines. I'd like to thank all the people who contributed to the Consultation on Urban Mission, in London during September 1985, for helping me to clarify my own thoughts on the subject.

Finally, we are indebted to those who read the typescript in draft form, and made many useful comments. These have included Dave Greenwood, John Pearce, Steve Cox, Kevin Coleman, Jenny Brailsford, and Vernon Angel. Any opinions expressed are naturally those of the authors.

Mike Fearon
London, May 1986

Foreword

by Christopher Idle

This book will provoke some mixed responses from those who venture beyond its opening pages.

There are still many people for whom the world described here is strange, alien, almost unbelievable; for them, some of Pete and Mike's conclusions may seem equally bizarre. For other readers, the bad news here will be all too familiar, the good news all too rare.

It is vital that those in the first group do not close their minds to what these pages are saying. If they do, they will remain both ignorant and deprived; ignorant of what is happening in today's cities, and deprived of a wealth of transforming love which is daily in operation wherever the Church of Jesus Christ is tackling its job locally.

It is also essential for the second group not to be discouraged because their own efforts do not measure up to the commitment, resilience, and spiritual stamina shown here – often indirectly and all the more powerfully for that. The book was not written to make us feel guilty; but the sense of responsibility which both sets of readers may experience can be healthy if it leads to action.

There are rough edges to these stories, to the people in them, and to the principles being worked out through them. That is because it is a real human document, not a glossy brochure; East London life is often untidy. Patterns shift even as a book like this is being put together; Church leaders sometimes have to change direction fast – and not just when they are being chased by a bunch of skinheads with broken bottles! Any account drawing neat, consistent conclusions would be a lie. Like the New Testament itself, Pete's and Mike's book gives us the facts, but also leaves us asking crucial questions rather than knowing all the answers. It is not written for entertainment or Christian titillation.

Above all, this is not the account of some eccentric, marginal piece of work on the sidelines of the Church's main activities. It is not a project completed as part of someone's research; it is not a brief hit-and-run experiment conducted by fringe characters; it is not a phase in the training of leaders who do their 'urban' stint as a preparation for moving on to something grander.

It is not even just an account of 'the way we live now', here is the mainstream of the Church's life, the heart of God's mission and ours in Britain today. We shall be wise to listen; supremely privileged to take part.

PART ONE

1
WASTAGE

I just couldn't believe it!

It had all started off like any other Monday evening. I'd opened up for the regular youth club that night, and all around me pool, table-tennis and all the other activities were getting into full swing.

Even when Keith Griffiths (the local London City Missioner) walked in,. I thought nothing much of it; Keith is a not-infrequent visitor to the club.

There was, perhaps, a certain sympathetic glint in his eye as he called me to one side, but nothing to prepare me for the news he'd brought.

"Did you hear about Tom Campbell?" he asked, tentatively, like a swimmer testing the water.

"I'm waiting for him to come in," I said. I'd arranged to meet Tom later that evening. So why had Keith come round to see me? Surely Tom could have waited to tell me any news himself.

"I've got some bad news, Pete," Keith said. He knew that there was no point in beating about the bush; that I'd rather he came straight out and told me. "I'm afraid Tom's dead. He's been murdered."

Tom? Dead? No, I just couldn't take this in.

"But I saw him only last Wednesday," I said in stunned disbelief. He'd been his usual aggressive self. But now he was gone; blown out as one more casualty on the battlefield of inner-city life.

In my role as an East End youth worker in a church-sponsored youth club, I live with the knowledge that people have to be saved urgently. I never know when I'll see them again. People in Hackney are so unpredictable; .

13

they might never come back to the club, or go near any church again.

Tom's death seemed so cheap. It brought home the reality of inner-city life in a sickening way. I felt absolutely gutted.

Ashen, I turned to Nick Simpson, a co-worker at the club: "Did I tell him?" I asked. Did I make it plain to Tom about Jesus? Did he decide ... no! .... *Did he have a chance* to decide? I just didn't know. I just knew that I'd never have another chance to explain.

"That's Tom," the friend had said who'd first pointed him out to me. "He's a loony." The first thing I ever saw him do was pick a fight with someone he felt had insulted him. He knocked the guy clean off the wall on which he was sitting.

After that, I'd see Tom fairly often. I'd take him aside and talk to him. I even invited him around to my flat, and that just wasn't done with Tom; he was a thief, so no one trusted him. But he never, ever stole anything from me.

He was the middle child in a large family. His parents couldn't cope, so Tom had been put in a home, at the age of eight. Thereafter, he'd always felt rejected. After he came out of the home, he used to try to win his family's love and respect by bringing luxury items into the home. But they were always stolen goods. The police would come, and the family would be nicked for receiving.

Tom had a heart of gold really. He was always willing to pitch into a fight to help out a mate. He desperately wanted to please those around him.

Then, a couple of nights before I was due to meet him, he went out for a few drinks with a mate. Returning to the guy's home, they got into an argument in the kitchen. Tom picked up a knife ...

Someone else in the house jumped Tom from behind. With a pair of bicycle handlebars that were at hand, they began hitting Tom over the head. I don't suppose they'd intended to hit him so hard but – by the time they'd finished – he was lying in a pool of blood, his head smashed in.

The killer was caught and sent to prison for three years. Three years, for killing someone! Sure, there were reasons: the court decided that it was a provoked attack; Tom had a police record for robbery and violence; and there were no witnesses to the incident. But it seemed like a funny sort of justice to me; eighteen months later, the killer was on the streets again, on parole.

As for Tom, in life he'd had nothing and in death he had nothing. No one had ever given him a chance to be different – except for a few Christians perhaps. But the Gospel message had apparently gone in one ear and out of the other; his problems distracted him from hearing. Tom was a product of his environment.

Jerry was one of Tom's contemporaries. He was a black guy; unemployed. He played for the youth club's football team, when he wasn't thieving. He was quite successful as a burglar.

One Wednesday, I had a long chat with him at the club, about God. After a lot of effort, I really felt that I was starting to get through to him. I was looking forward to seeing him on Saturday, at the football match. I was itching to continue our discussion where we'd left off.

On the Friday, Jerry was 'doing a job'. He smashed a window to break into a house. But, as he was climbing through, he ripped his stomach open on the jagged glass at the bottom of the window frame. He died in the hallway of some stranger's home. The first I heard about it was when he didn't turn up to play football.

Bobby was a different sort of casualty. He was a drug addict. I've lost count of the number I've met like him. Many of them are now dead, but Bobby survived because of an encounter with the police. He went up to Leicester with his brother and, within a week, he'd been arrested for armed robbery. At our club, it's not an infrequent event to hear about armed robberies. Burglaries are so commonplace that no one really pays any attention to stories about them any longer.

In prison, Bobby was brought down off drugs. There

are others I've known who have not been so fortunate. Jane was another of the lucky ones. She came into the club stoned out of her mind; I took her up to Hackney hospital to be stomach-pumped, and saved her life.

Another guy I took to be stomach-pumped resented me for it afterwards. If I hadn't he'd have been lying on a mortuary slab, but his only response was to complain, "You've just taken away my weekend 'buzz'." He'd taken so many narcotics that he'd expected to be high all weekend. Now that they'd all been pumped out of him, he didn't know what to do with all that spare time!

It hurts me to see young, healthy people abusing their bodies and throwing their lives away. It's the Indians and Pakistanis for whom I really feel sorry. They always seem to be the 'fall guys' whenever one of the local thugs feels that he's got something to prove. People of different nationalities and different backgrounds have different ways of life. But some of the bully boys in Hackney can't accept that it's quite alright for people to be different from one another. They always want to prove that their way of doing things is better than everyone else's. It's often the Asian population that becomes the innocent target of victimisation and bullying. Funnily enough, it's usually the other black kids that pick on the Asians. There's as much prejudice, for example, between the Afro-Caribbeans and Asians, as there is between blacks and whites.

Most of the fights that we get in the club are not between different cultures, or even amongst males of the same culture. It's usually the girls, rather than the guys, who want to fight. I can always tell when there's going to be trouble; there's a tension in the air. Word goes around that, say, two girls have been in an argument at school. Everyone's waiting for them to come into the club. I know when the fight's about to start, because everyone heads for the door. They all want a good view when the girls go for one another outside.

The last time that it happened, one girl didn't want to fight but the other one did. It didn't make any difference;

16

she was still slapped and hit.

"Look, she doesn't want to fight!" I said to her assailant. "You've won! What are you trying to prove?"

"I wanna hurt her! I wanna hurt her!"

I jumped in and pulled them apart. As everyone trooped back into the club, it was clear that I wasn't popular for spoiling the 'entertainment'.

These people all have one thing in common. They are all examples of wasted lives that need not be that way. There are many other young people who trod the same road, but who were able to change direction for the better. Christians in the inner-city can act like road signs, to guide people towards a better way of life. But it requires perseverance and a willingness to become available in the lives of the community and the individuals within it.

A group of people involved in evangelism amongst young people met for discussions at the NIE (National Initiative in Evangelism) assembly in 1980. They concluded that areas like Hackney, that are socially, culturally and educationally deprived,

> bear the brunt of truancy, unemployment and delinquency among the 14-22 age range. Such young people experience deeper deprivation and alienation than most sectors of the community. They are unskilled or semi-skilled . . . They are often at odds with themselves, with society and with God.

I know that it's true, because I've seen it with my own eyes in the lives of those around me. I've introduced you to some of them in this chapter. Hopelessness is written across their faces; hopelessness that stems largely from powerlessness. The young generation in the inner-city is in control of *nothing*; not even its own destiny. People are living in a vacuum, but have become too apathetic to be concerned about their plight. To quote from a Sex Pistols' song: "We're vacant, and we don't care!"

Part of the problem stems from a lack of basic amenities. Hackney, and particularly Homerton – the part of the borough where my youth club is situated – is very poorly served by public transport. The borough, in 1986, had one of the highest unemployment rates of any borough in the entire British Isles, so most people are without their own transport; though that's only one of the basic facilities that they're lacking, in the poverty trap.

We are fortunate in having more open space than is available, say, down at the Bethnal Green end of Hackney. But the space is not particularly usable. We have Hackney Marshes, an uncultivated, semi-wilderness that is of little use to anyone. There are fields on which young people can kick a football about, but that quickly becomes facile. There is no education about how to *use* the available space, any more than there is about how to use the empty time that trickles through the fingers of most of the dole queue kids.

Deprivation is another factor in the problem. Colin Marchant, in his book *Signs in the City*, hit the nail on the head when he said:

> Deprivation is an unpleasant word for an ugly reality. It has to do with taking away. It is a denial, a removal, a withdrawal and a withholding. This deprivation is known as unemployment, poor housing, a drab environment and a general lack of choice. It leads to disadvantage and distress and ends in despair and want.

It is a major cause of human wastage in the inner-city.

Those who have to endure these conditions while passing through adolescence and early adulthood are doubly disadvantaged. Youth is a rehearsal for maturity; and the pains and traumas of acne; the first period, discovering one's sexual identity, achieving a sense of belonging, developing appropriate dependance patterns, and the other phenomena of development into adulthood are disturbing enough within a sympathetic environment, but faced with the inner-city they are many times more disturbing. It is against this backdrop that my club operates.

What are our club sessions like? If you came along one evening, you'd find yourself at a one-storey, red-brick, pre-war building in a side street about two hundred yards from Hackney Hospital. The building is perhaps sixty feet long by thirty feet wide, with a yard at the back surrounded by a fifteen-foot fence. (The ball still goes over the top, or over the club roof, when the members get too enthusiastic.) The main hall takes up about two-thirds of the space inside, with a coffee-bar occupying most of the remainder – though it can be divided into two rooms with a wooden screen when needed. The other rooms are minute, and comprise an office, a couple of storage cupboards, a small balcony, a kitchen store room, WCs and showers. I think the office is probably the smallest room in the building; it's about the size of a large WC cubicle!

The first thing that you would notice, before you even got through the door, would be the steady throb of music. The hi-fi is usually run flat out all evening, with the volume so high that it distorts. All you can hear is the rhythm, pounding out like some huge industrial machine throbbing away. Sometimes it's 'scratch reggae'; other times, it may be a 'disco rap'. It's seldom chart material.

Once inside, you'd notice that the majority of members are black. They eye up strangers and newcomers with suspicion. For all they know, you might be a police officer. But after a few minutes they start to relax. They may ask you what you're doing, or simply challenge you to a game of table-tennis. There's usually a queue waiting to use the pool tables.

People ask me how youth work can stem the flow of wasted lives. It can't! People need to be changed from the *inside*, in their whole outlook, values and attitudes. They need to be completely transformed, and only Jesus can do that. Youth work provides a setting in which that can happen – and in which young people can develop and grow.

You can't say to someone who's been unemployed for ten years, "Here's a job; get on with it," and expect his life to change overnight. It's stupid. They need to be shown how to live their lives, all over again. They need a new zest for living, a belief that life is livable, and the knowledge that there's an answer to it all. It's a lifestyle that has nothing to do with work or possessions, but which concerns itself with having a purpose, a reason to live. All that I can offer as a youth worker is to be a living signpost, pointing to God – the one who alone can fill all the empty spaces in people's lives.

Secular youth work is really nothing more than a holding operation, striving to stop matters from getting worse. But most youth agencies close their doors on Friday and Saturday nights – the nights when most kids are on the streets, desperate for something to do. The summer holidays, when those at school have six weeks to spend in leisure, is the very time when most youth workers take their own holidays! But these are the very times when my church-affiliated youth club opens its doors most frequently, with a 'holiday-club' project. I'm a Christian first, and a youth worker second. It's not what I *do* that matters; it's what I *am* that counts.

Many young people today seem beyond the reach of the churches. There is a failure to share the good news with these people. The Church has failed to understand and respond to the distinctive 'youth culture' that has emerged since the 1950s. At the same time, due to deprivation, poverty and powerlessness, our urban areas are in turmoil. In combination, these factors have given rise to a spiritual watershed in the inner-city. Yet they are not two distinct problems, but rather, different manifestations of the one: a failure to communicate.

We need to develop a setting for communication to take place. We need to explore the common ground of our shared humanity, our feelings, thoughts, needs and concerns. Christians need to identify with the oppressed; to share the same job centres, snack-bars and street corners. We need to humble ourselves and ask God to change us, in order that we might conform to Christ the Suffering Servant who identified with the suffering of mankind.

There is light at the end of the tunnel. Many Christians I know are beginning to interpret our faith in ways which reach our contemporaries, through the secular media, through a distinctive lifestyle, and through caring for the needs of particular, oppressed sections of society – including young people, through youth work. Pray God, more Christians will catch the vision and respond to the need.

2

A DAY AT A TIME

I was once asked how many hours per day a Christian youth worker should spend in prayer. I hope that I won't be considered too impious for my job if I confess that three-quarters of an hour is usually about my lot! I try to rise at about 6.20 a.m., and I have 'until my children wake up' to spend with the Lord. The noisy patter of feet usually disturbs my meditation just after 7.00 a.m. In that short time, I usually aim to sit in thought for a few minutes – with a cup of tea to stop me from nodding off – before I let my thoughts focus themselves into prayers. My quiet time ends with reading a few verses from Scripture, which tend to be curtailed by cries of 'Dad! Dad!' from the children coming down the stairs.

For the next few hours, my life revolves around Mark and Jamie. I'll play with them and their toys, or perhaps watch TV or a video. I would never dream of sticking my head in a newspaper in front of them, any more than I would dream of being so rude with an adult visitor.

It's too easy for youth workers to neglect their wives; they forget that, when they marry, they become one flesh. My wife, Anne, comes down a little later than the boys and we have breakfast before Mark, who's now five, goes off to school. I believe that it's up to me to outdo myself in putting my wife first in everything, just as I come first in her life. Anne is usually back from taking Mark to school just before I leave for work, at about 9.45 a.m.

I usually get to my office at about ten o'clock. That makes it sound as though I'm one of the pin-stripe suit and bowler hat brigade; but I'm more likely to be wearing jeans, sweat-shirt and training-shoes. After another cup of tea (I never drink coffee) I'm ready to take a look at the post.

What comes next depends on whether or not there's a meeting that morning. We have full-time workers' meetings, area meetings, church staff meetings, and our own staff meetings. In an average month, I've probably got between seven and ten meetings to attend in connection with the club, and probably the same number in connection with church business. On top of that, I have individual sessions with all the part-time staff on a monthly basis, as part of my supervisory role. At present, I've also got a student from the YMCA training-school working in the club; I meet with him weekly.

Of all the meetings, the Tuesday morning sessions that I have with the full-time workers are easily the most important. At present, there are two other full-time workers at the club, with one more to be appointed imminently. But two of the part-time staff have given up their day jobs to give all their attention over to youth work, and they usually join us, too.

The format we're aiming for with these three-hour meetings is: one hour where we each talk about ourselves in relation to the work of the club; an hour or more general sharing where we talk about any personal problems, and 'where we're at as Christians'; and an hour where we turn to God, through Bible study and/or prayer. A variety of topics gets covered at these meetings. For example, at our last meeting we discussed the problem of members drinking alcohol and smoking dope in the club. We don't allow this, but the problem is how to stop it.

Aside from meetings, I've always got other work to do, to think about, or to organise. It may be writing letters, buying equipment, preparing for meetings, or writing a talk for the Sunday or Wednesday epilogue. Cleaning is usually done by one of the part-time workers, to earn a little extra cash. I'm a bit of a jack-of-all-trades, and I seem to get involved in everything from going to court to give a character-witness for members who've got into trouble with the police, to getting hold of a van to help someone to move into a flat.

My afternoons are sacred. From 1.00 p.m. till 5.00 p.m., I will not have anything to do with youth work unless I can't get out of it. That's the time that I spend with my wife and family; though I do often make phone calls in the afternoon, on behalf of the club, but against my better judgement. I work in the club all evening when many families have the freedom to gather together to do as they wish. For me, the afternoon is the time when I do whatever most families would do of an evening. It's worth saying again: it's too easy for youth workers to neglect their own families. Here I am, doing the work that God wants me to do, helping young people to develop and to grow; but I'd be a hypocrite if I didn't take the time out to do those things with my own family too.

Fridays and Saturdays are my days off, but we seldom go away anywhere. Holidays and day-trips are not my scene; I'd much rather invite some friends around for a meal, a Bible study, or just for a chat. People often have a go at me for not going away on long holidays. I'm entitled to seven weeks paid leave each year, but I never take more than two or three weeks. (Before I married, I never took *any* holiday!) I enjoy my work, and I enjoy my days off, but it's all anyone can do to chase me out of Hackney for a couple of weeks at a holiday camp each year. That's gradually beginning to change, and I find myself beginning to take more and more of my holiday entitlement each year, to spend with my family.

Before I married, I thrived on youth work as an all-day job. It was very difficult to make the adjustment when I got married, and had responsibility for a wife. I hadn't the freedom to keep 'doing my own thing'. I had to change my work patterns. I think it's wonderful that single people, if they wish, can choose to work a twelve or fifteen-hour day (a bit like a vicar!) and to make incredible progress in their work. But you can only keep it up for a few years, or you start to burn out. Better to cut back to more sensible hours, and have the stamina to keep at the job for a lifetime.

On Mondays, the *real* youth work starts at 5.00 p.m., with the Junior Club (five to twelve-year-olds). That's mainly physical activity, with the kids running around enjoying themselves. We encourage games that involve them in physical activity with each other. They don't have much opportunity for that in the East End, where often the macho he-man image permits two males to touch each other only when they're belting the hell out of one another with their fists. The non-verbal affection of simply holding hands in a circle can be a powerful antidote to the godless insensitivity of the inner-city.

At 6.30 p.m. two experienced hockey players arrive to tutor some of the older youngsters in this popular sport. It's quite a mixed group of Asians, Afro-Caribbeans and whites; about fifteen of them in all. In the main hall, we have circuit training running simultaneously with weight-training in the back room.

At 8.00 p.m., the Senior Club arrives. Two pool tables and three or four table-tennis tables come into use. The members often bring in records or – mainly – tapes of their favourite music; usually ethnic sounds such as 'dub reggae'. Me and the other workers mix in with the multi-racial young people, sometimes playing a game of table-tennis, or running a football or basketball match outside, on the floodlit yard, but primarily just being there to relate to the members. We hope they feel that they can use us as sounding boards, off which to bounce ideas; as counsellors, in whom they can confide their problems; as advisors – sometimes even as careers officers! – who can give them information and guidance; and, hopefully, as friends whom they can trust, and whose company they can enjoy.

Tuesday evenings are given over to the Junior Club and the 'Inters' – those aged intermediately between

25

Junior and Senior clubs. The programme there consists of energetic, physical games – often of a highly competitive nature.

On Wednesdays, we hold a prayer meeting from 6.00 to 7.00 p.m., before starting up the club with a programme similar to that of Monday, except that the session goes on for an extra half-hour, and is punctuated with a short talk in the middle. One week, the talk was prefaced by my turning off the music at the master switch, with a special key. After getting the members' attention, I proceeded to show how I could turn the lights on and off with the key, in the same way. "This key", I said, "can leave you in darkness, or plunge you into light. Your spiritual life has a key, too. You can remain spiritually in the dark, or you can step on out into the light. The key that can do that for you is Jesus." It was a bit corny, and there were some smiles from club members; but it was a simple message, and it got through to the young people at their own level.

Thursday sees the club open specifically for girls, who often find it daunting to have to mix with rough lads, though some of them *do* come on other nights too. Their programme varies towards more obviously feminine activities – such as rounders, sewing and netball – though they also play pool, table-tennis, and even football. They can do all these without fear of being laughed at by males. Once each month, there is a special staff/ members meeting that night – for all the members – when they can have the opportunity to feed back new ideas for activities that they'd like to see introduced into the programme. We have some good rows, and we have some good discussions; but it all makes them feel a part of the club, that they can say 'we want this and we want that'.

Friday and Saturday evenings, the club is usually closed, though there is a playgroup for the under fives on the Friday morning, and Vernon – a part-time worker – runs football coaching on Saturday mornings. At the moment, there's also a session of Taekwondo training (a

26

form of martial art) – with an outside coach – on Friday evenings.

Sunday is our Senior Club again, from 7.00 to 10.00 p.m. On the first Sunday of each month, there is a special evangelistic service slotted into the evening, for about a half-hour, beginning at 8.30 p.m. We've found it difficult to maintain any kind of thoughtful reflection once the club starts again at 9.00 p.m., and it would be better from that respect if the service could be the last item of the evening. But, if we did that, the kids would soon cotton on and leave the club before the service began. As it is, they all stay around and watch, because they know they've got another hour for games afterwards.

During all the youth club sessions, I 'muck in' with the other workers, chatting with the members, playing them at pool or arranging a football session in the yard outside. I'm not the sort of youth worker who walks around with a big bunch of keys, or who spends all evening sitting in the office. I don't let any of my Christian co-workers sit in the office either; if they've any administration to do, they do it during the day. When the club's running, they're there to work, and they get out and do it – by talking with the young people and instigating activities.

The schedule means that I'm unable to attend Sunday evening service at church; I can only manage morning worship. I exempt myself from the club on Tuesday evenings to charge off to the House Group that I lead. It's fortunate that I'm not needed that night. Being the Junior Club, there aren't the problems of keeping the members under control in the same way that we sometimes have with the Senior Club. Our two part-time workers are able to manage the Junior Club by themselves, which means that they are able to take on more responsibility than they would have if I was present to sort out any difficulties that might arise!

On an average night, there may be forty or fifty members in the club, but it only needs a light shower of rain near opening time for two-thirds of them to stay at home. We're under no illusions that the club – for most of them – is anything other than just 'somewhere to go'. They come in because it's better than standing around on a street corner. Inside, people relate in isolated groups. They wander around with no great expectations of having a good time; they're just glad to be in the company of their friends.

No one really says what they mean. Many don't mean what they say. Everyone hides behind a front. I came across a monologue recently which, for me, puts into words everything that I believe these young people are feeling, but dare not admit. I don't know who wrote it.

Don't be fooled by me.
Don't be fooled by the mask that I wear,
for I wear a thousand masks, masks that I'm afraid to take off,
and none of them are me.
Pretending is an art that's second nature to me,
but don't be fooled.
I give the impression that I'm secure;
that all is sunny and unruffled with me, within me as well as without,
that confidence is my name and coolness my game,
that the water is wide and I'm in command,
and that I need no one.
But don't believe me. Please . . .

I chatter idly to you in the suave tones of surface talk.
I tell you everything that is really nothing,
and nothing of what's everything.
I dislike the superficial game I'm playing. The phoney game.
But the nearer you approach me, the blinder I strike back.
I fight against the very thing that I cry out for.
But love is stronger than walls, and in this lies my hope.
Who am I, you may wonder.
I am someone you know very well.
I am every man you meet, and I am every woman you meet.

I know a thing or two about masks. I've hidden behind plenty of them in my youth. When I was born, in 1950, I was the last of three brothers. I suppose my parents had really been hoping for a girl, so I was probably a disappointment to them from the beginning. When my sister came along a couple of years later, she and I shared the same bedtimes, when I wanted to go to bed at the same time as my brothers. I suppose that's when the first mask appeared, to hide my feelings of worthlessness.

I seemed to get my older brothers' hand-me-downs, as happens in most large families. Only my plimsoles (or training-shoes as they call them now) were bought new. Even so, they didn't stay new for long. With my constantly playing football in them, there would soon be holes through the soles, and I had to keep putting cardboard in them to cover the holes.

On one occasion, I went to a cinema in near-by Chatsworth Road – called The Castle – wearing plimsoles in this condition. Unfortunately, it was raining heavily and my feet soon became soaked. The patched jeans and flimsy shirt I was wearing gave little protection either. Soon I was soaked to the skin. I couldn't get any wetter, so I began jumping in puddles and splashing about. It was a bit like the famous sequence from the show *Singing in the Rain*!

When I finally reached the cinema and met my mates outside, I was eager to get in and get dried out. We never used to pay to get in. We'd always 'bunk in' as we called it. One of us would distract the cashier while the rest of us ran inside. We always timed it so that the lights had gone down and the adverts which preceded the main film were being shown. That way, even if we were noticed and pursued, the management wouldn't be able to spot us in the darkness.

After we came out of our 'free' film show, we played a quick game of football before it got dark. It was still raining and, though I'd dried out in the cinema, I was soon soaked again. But I was young and happy; what did I care?

Next morning though, I began to regret my foolhardy behaviour. Boy, was I ill! I was sweating, running a temperature, and delirious. Mum called the doctor, and he diagnosed pneumonia. I spent the next six weeks in hospital where, for the first time in my life, there were people around who really took some notice of me. The nurses pampered me in a way that my parents – with three other children – were never able to do.

For a month afterwards, I had to stay in the house, and a district nurse would come around to give me daily injections. I was embarrassed at having to take my pants down while the lady jabbed her needle in my bum! I soon realised that she always came at near enough the same time each day; so I would always run and hide when I knew she was due. I'd scamper into the toilet and lock the door behind me.

My mum would sit outside and talk with the nurse, until eventually I thought they'd forgotten about me. My inquisitiveness would get the better of me, so I'd sneak down to try to eavesdrop. Then they'd grab me, my pants would come down, and the nurse would come towards me with the big needle. My bum was like a pin-cushion in the end.

Eventually, I was allowed out of the house again, and I could go back to school. Not long afterwards, I moved on to secondary school at Upton House. They let me play football for the school but, because my name was Stow, I wasn't encouraged to do much else. One of my brothers had been at the school for two years, and had acquired a reputation as a bit of a 'hard-case'. The teachers expected me to try to follow in his footsteps, and were determined that I wouldn't succeed. "We know you. You're this sort of person," the teachers assumed. "You can't do this; you mustn't do that; and we'll cane you if you do the other." I was pigeon-holed before I'd even been given an opportunity to break the stereotype.

That's not to say that I was an angel. I can remember, at the age of ten, sitting in my classroom in trepidation because another boy whom I'd hardly beaten up was being brought around to all the classrooms to try to identify his assailant. As the boy looked around the classroom, I tried to look away; but our eyes suddenly met, and I saw the gleam of recognition dart across his face. I was picked out and caned, though – perversely – they also gave me a place in the school boxing team!

At secondary school, my only interests were football and fighting. I was an angry, frustrated young eastender. At the age of twelve, I rescued my fourteen-year-old brother from a fight, and bashed up his fifteen-year-old opponent. I'd acquired a reputation as a good fighter; in fact, I'd never lost a fight to anyone.

Branded a trouble maker, the whole of my secondary education was spent in the lowest stream. Though Upton House was supposed to be a comprehensive school with no inequalities in education, the pupils in the upper stream received the attention of the best-qualified and most-able teachers. In the lower streams, we got the teachers who couldn't care less. All the comprehensive system did for me was to enforce the differences. I gradually became more and more indifferent to my schooling. Increasingly, I developed a chip on my shoulder and a grudge against society.

So, you see, one reason why I can relate well to the embittered young people at our youth club is that, twenty years ago, I myself used to be just the way they are now. If it wasn't for the local Christians who saw through the mask that I wore – who showed me how to love and to be loved – I would be just the way their parents often are; I'd be too preoccupied with my own concerns and miseries to bring them up properly.

But becoming a Christian changed my life. A typical day in my life now is very different from a typical day from my childhood, or a day in the lives of our members' parents. It's only the kids who haven't changed. Their lives are no different from my childhood days.

No different at all . . .

3

OPEN YOUTH WORK

I'd never seen anyone run so fast in my life!

There he went, scampering up the road with me and my mates in pursuit, all armed with clubs, broken bottles or metal combs sharpened into deadly weapons.

It's not every church youth worker who can say that he once chased a curate up the street, trying to cut him up!

It happened like this. I was still at school at the time, though very rebellious and resentful of authority. I didn't relate well to any of the teachers. Religious Education had always seemed a totally irrelevant subject – even more so than the others – until a new RE teacher arrived. Clive Skinner was his name; a youngish guy, with a thin face and a big nose. Our previous RE teachers had always talked about the Bible as though it were just an old history book. I hated it.

Clive though, had other ideas about how to communicate the truths of Christianity. He radiated a real friendliness; there was no fear in him. I really felt that he *cared* about the class, and that – even when he addressed the whole class – he was still talking to me personally.

We'd all expected him to hand out Bibles to us but, instead, he gave out copies of a paperback book entitled *The Cross and the Switchblade*, about David Wilkerson's ministry to the street-gangs in New York. It's a bit dated now, but in those days it seemed really gripping. It was really relevant to the kind of life we were living.

Clive would read it out loud, while the rest of us followed in our own copies. He clearly understood that most of us had difficulty with reading, even in our early teens. But we kept the books in our desks between lessons, so that we could try to read the story for ourselves, if we wished.

After one RE lesson, I talked to Clive about the skinhead gang to which I belonged. I was starting to feel like an English Nicky Cruz – a violent character in the book. Clive kept inviting me along to his church on Sundays. It was embarrassing initially, but eventually I went along to see what it was like. I felt in awe at first, I'd gone there of my own free will, and I really felt that God was there.

John Pearce, the vicar, made my mates and me feel very welcome. It was a very high church service there, at the time, but it didn't matter – the congregation made me feel a part of the service.

I became involved with the youth club simply because it was there. Another night, I'd go along to the mid-week Bible study. But the rest of the time I'd be out with my mates, getting drunk or taking drugs. There never seemed to me to be any contradiction in that. I used to play drums in the special youth services, but I'd down a whole bottle of cider first, to give me some Dutch-courage.

There must have been about thirty of us, my mates and me. When we started going to the youth club, there were other kids already using the premises; but we couldn't have that. After a few rows and fights, all the original members left and we were there in their place. We had a real feeling of belonging. It was an ordinary drab church hall with very little equipment, but at least we had a place of our own where we could meet. That was important to us because, previously, we'd had to meet out on street corners, trying to keep dry when it rained.

Though I had become a church-goer, I certainly wasn't a Christian. Looking back recently, John Pearce described me as "one of a gang of tearaways who were always involved in all kinds of trouble. In fact, some of them were even involved in a murder around that time."

In short, I once belonged to the sort of group with which I now work. I could very easily have gone down the same road as those 'casualties' that I described in the first chapter.'

It was inevitable, living that kind of double-life, that the situation would eventually explode. The crunch came one night when Ted Longman, the curate, organised an event for the club in the old church hall. My mates and I were there, pretending to be tough. The event took the form of a concert by a Christian band with a lot of flashy equipment. We didn't like that. The presence of all the equipment, and the attitude of the band – which we felt to be of superiority – brought out all of our own inadequacies. We felt threatened.

Tension mounted, and eventually erupted when someone waved a broken bottle in front of Ted's face. Ted put up his hands to defend himself, and his assailant fell backwards. We hadn't seen the bottle incident and so, to us, it looked as though the curate had provoked the fight. The band's equipment was badly damaged in the ensuing fracas. Ted escaped out of the door; someone shouted, "He's getting away!" We all chased after him, throwing bricks and yelling out. Needless to say, after that, it was the end of going to church for me. I felt that I'd gone too far – been too bad. Surely God wouldn't want anything to do with me after that.

That was back in 1967. It's ironical that the youth club which my mates and I stormed out of should be the very same youth club where I'm now employed as Senior Youth Worker!

But what went wrong? Why did that flare-up occur to separate me from the Church back in the mid-sixties? John believes that, at that time, my friends and I had grown out of youth clubs and were into something a good deal more violent. But perhaps the real reason was that the church was unable to operate a youth club that would appeal to the sort of rowdy, aggressive teenager that I'd become.

The kind of club which I run now is the sort that caters for young people who have been thrown out of conventional youth clubs. There are two basic types of youth work undertaken in churches: open and closed. Examples of closed youth work situations – which cater mainly for children and young people from a Christian background – include Cubs, Scouts, Pathfinders, Boys Brigade, Crusaders, Girl Guides, Church Youth Fellowship Association (CYFA), etc. Well run, these can be extremely effective. They cater mainly for conservative, controlled youngsters, who need the safety net of a set of rules and regulations.

Open youth work caters for young people who have no church connections, and who probably know next to nothing about Christianity. Open youth work means going out on a limb; which is probably why so few churches attempt it. It involves taking risks, and accepting people who, perhaps, have been rejected by other youth clubs because of their violent behaviour.

Too often, the Church isn't interested in the outcast or loud-mouthed person of whom the secular youth clubs wish to be rid. But this is exactly the sort of person in whom Christ would probably have taken a special interest. Too often, we Christians are too busy being 'religious', instead of getting to know our own day's equivalent of the tax-collectors, prostitutes, Samaritans and lepers. In many Christian circles, the wild, un-churched young person has metaphorically had his card stamped with 'failure'; but Christian open youth work gives everyone a tick. If that person wants to give him/herself a bad mark, it's their choice. But, as Christians, it's our job to give them the tick first.

The aim of all youth work is *growth*. One of my former colleagues, Peter Ellem, defines it as "Getting young people to grow in confidence, and in their ability to understand themselves and the events that are going on around them. Successful youth work enables young people to feel that they matter – that they have a part to play in society."

This 'growth' is not necessarily growth to fit in with society. It is growth to make a choice – whether to fit in with the social system in the normal way, or whether to adopt a different lifestyle of their own. If that sounds very radical, it should be remembered that a true *Christian* lifestyle is very different from society's norm.

Another former colleague, Sue Gibbson, says that, "A second purpose is to enable young people to build relationships with adults and people who are not part of their everyday lives. Youth workers (professional or otherwise) pass on their skills, knowledge and understanding by sharing these with the young people, in order to give them a different viewpoint. Often, young people only meet the same sort of adult – parents, relations, school teachers, etc. A youth worker helps a young person to find a more balanced picture of society. It puts them in a position where they can make choices for themselves."

The spiritual side of growth is too often ignored in schools and secular youth clubs. It often comes as a shock to young people to realise that there *is* a God; there is *meaning*; there is *purpose* to life. Christian open youth work must aim to cater for the whole person. Statutory (state-run) youth work caters for the physical and mental needs of young people, but church-based youth work adds an extra, spiritual dimension, without neglecting the other two areas of need.

Though Britain is nominally a Christian country, I find that many young people these days have very little knowledge of Christianity. Strangely, the country's black population – particularly West Indian – are often more knowledgeable than the whites! But their conception of God is usually a very legalistic one.

For example, a lad called Simon came into the club the other night, and said that – if we were real Christians – we should not allow smoking in the club, and should refuse admission to anyone who smoked or took drugs. If we did that, we'd have to ban 90 per cent of our membership! It was obvious that Simon had a very repressed view of God. In his mind, being a Christian meant keeping a whole series of rules – do this, do that, don't go there, come here – rather than having a living relationship with God.

Many older people still stand for God, while younger people rebel against him, believing him to be just another example of all that their parents represent. God is seen, mistakenly, as being part of the package of rules and regulations to which they are expected to *conform*, without having any *power* or real say in what goes on. They find that they have no equality with their parents, but feel only the *imposing* factor of religion. Christian open youth work must first aim to take away the imposition, before being in a position to present the gospel.

I believe that this can be done in several ways, and allowing a group to make some of its own decisions is often a good start. It gives the young people some real power; even if the decisions they take are comparatively minor. Attention to individuals is an important aspect, particularly if certain people have special problems – shyness for example. Power can be conferred by allowing individual members to introduce particular topics in discussions. (They may need to be shown the best way of doing this; rather than to simply say, "Tonight's topic is so-and-so, what do you think of it?" and having utter silence ensue, it's often better to make a provocative statement, showing a picture/film, or play a topical record.) Outings, residential weekends and holidays, when the leaders can be seen as real people – and when there is more time available than in a two-hour club session – can be good times to break down barriers.

I find that, often, young people feel that adults repress them and refuse to let them have their own way, out of malice. A common complaint is that their parents won't let them watch the programmes that they want to see on TV. It doesn't occur to them that perhaps their parents genuinely want to watch a programme on the other channel, and that the parents are not being unreasonable. But the young people quickly realise their mistake when they come to the club and want to watch a programme while other members are watching another channel! In that situation, it's clearly the members of their own peer group who are preventing them from having their own way. They quickly realise that they can't always watch what they want to watch; to achieve their own way, they have to resort to politeness, reason and gentle persuasion. Many gradually realise that their sense of repression in the home is due simply to different people having different views.

When I take young people away for a weekend, we always let *them* decide where we are going, and let them have a say in the organisation of rotas. "When we get there," I tell them, "there'll be no mum or dad to clear up after us, and I'm not going to do it." They have the power to do what they want to do, but they quickly learn that power brings with it responsibility. Once we've removed their ideas of being imposed upon in home life, any sense of God being just another adult with a set of rules is diminished too. The young people begin to see that, perhaps, they were wrong in their views about religion; but only if the standard of youth work has been good enough for the sense of oppression to be removed.

It is important, we find, that church youth work should be in no way inferior to the youth work provided by local authorities. Too many Christian youth groups, that I've seen, buy cheap and inferior equipment. But a young person, unless he/she is exceptionally rowdy, inevitably has a *choice* of youth clubs to which he/she she can go. If a secular youth club is providing better facilities, the young person would rather go there than to the church-run youth club.

In the Church Information Office publication *Bewildered but Believing*, it is stated that 'every parish needs to work out how it can help young people, whether they belong to the church or not. This should be done as part

38

of a policy thought out by the PCC.' Too often, youth work is seen as something which may be done by one or two members of the congregation, as long as it doesn't make demands on the rest of the church. This is wrong. It demonstrates a failure to grasp the biblical basics of youth work.

John 3:16 begins with the words 'For God loved the world so much . . .' But many Christians don't seem to *believe* that God loves the world in practice, and they don't seem to care for all types of people. Teenagers seem to be one type of people who have a bad reputation for over-indulging in sex, drugs and violence. Yet God loves them as much as the middle class, the elderly or young children. We should therefore spend a *proportion* of our time – and of our church's money and effort – in trying to win teenagers for Christ. Young people have particular needs, which often can't be met simultaneously with the more conservative needs of older people. Giving special attention to the different needs of different segments of society, one segment at a time, is simply a strategy for carrying out Christ's command to 'go into all the world'.

We don't find anywhere in the Bible that, for example, St Paul went to Ephesus and started a youth group. But Jesus clearly cared very much for the weak and powerless; and Paul's message was for those people – the gentiles – whom the Jews regarded as worthless.

In our society, one equivalent of the poor, the widowed, the childless and the Samaritan, whom Jesus cared for, is the young person. Young people can't vote. They are under their parents' thumb – or in council care – until they are sixteen. Once they begin work, always assuming that they can find a job, they find themselves at the very bottom of the promotion ladder, in the lowliest position. Jesus has a bias for the poor. As Christians, we should share his bias.

David Sheppard, in his book *Built as a City*, writes of a PCC that turned down an offer of a 100 per cent grant to pay for a qualified youth worker who would work in the parish. One member explained that the feelings which motivated the refusal were never really brought out into the open, but seemed to be that they didn't want the sort of kids that an open youth project was likely to attract on their church premises.

A church's youth policy often exposes the *fears* of its members; the fear that having young people in the church will bring down standards. Yes, groups of young people can present great problems to those with responsibilities for managing church halls; but let's not forget that people matter more than things.

Some churches insist on such standards of behaviour that many urban youngsters would never go near again. And that represents lost opportunity for leading young people into God's kingdom. How silly to worry about the church hall getting into a mess when God's got a new mansion waiting for each of us in his heavenly kingdom!

"If a church's youth work is run primarily for the young people who grew up through Sunday school, choir, Bible class or uniformed organisations, a social pattern will generally have appeared by the age of fourteen," says David Sheppard. Most of the people in the youth group will be those who have done well at school. Those who haven't done so well often feel that to join a Christian youth group means abandoning their mates and their culture. To do so makes them feel very insecure. In consequence, they give – not just the youth group – but the whole established Church a wide berth for the rest of their lives.

In spite of the arguments in favour of Christian open youth work, it's still practised far too infrequently in Britain today. There are two objections often raised by churches that are afraid of the concept. The first is: Why don't we read about it in the Bible? Why has it taken the Church 1,900 years to notice the need? My answer is that the need is a recent one, caused by an important change in society over the past 100 years – the virtual collapse of family life through the industrialisation of society.

Furthermore, the growth of the 'rock culture' in the last thirty years had hastened the end, and has led to the increasing alienation of young people from family life.

The youth culture as we now see it would have been totally foreign to anyone living before the Industrial Revolution. When an agricultural society existed – as in Christ's day, and as in Britain through to the nineteenth century – a person went straight from being a child to being a man without an intermediate stage of youth. As soon as the child could work in the field, he/she became a worker and was, as such, a valued member of the community. People usually married in their teens and were parents before they reached their twenties.

Even with the Industrial Revolution, children were working in factories or mines long before they reached their teens. They didn't hang around on street corners because they were working fourteen hours per day, and sleeping for most of the remaining ten.

But as society has become more mechanised, and the working week has become shorter, people have found more time on their hands. The raising of the school leaving age has meant that young people below the age of sixteen are occupied for only five or six hours per day, for five days per week, for less than forty weeks per year. They have more free time than ever before. These days, young people generally have more money and often more control over their own leisure. Youth work is needed to show them how to use that leisure time beneficially.

A second argument sometimes used against *Christian* youth work is: surely the State does enough already. The State undertakes a certain amount of work in financing and regulating youth clubs, under statutory provision. But it's controlled. A *voluntary* group, as most church-run youth groups invariably have to be, has the freedom to introduce the Christian faith into its activities. State-controlled youth work ignores the spiritual side of a young person. With the way RE is rapidly becoming forced out of state schools, it seems to be only a matter of

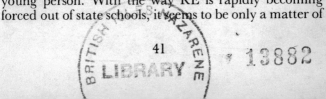

time before discussion of Christianity is actually prohibited in state-run youth clubs.

Even a voluntary group can benefit from State provision. At St Paul's, Homerton, the wages of three full-time and five part-time workers are paid by the Inner London Education Authority (ILEA). These Christians have been 'set free' from having to do a daytime job, and can conserve their energies for youth work of an evening. It is worth considering whether the Lord is calling for a similar scheme to be operated in your own church.

Because St Paul's youth club is voluntary, it can formulate its own programme. It can open when it likes, and do what it likes – in consultation with the statutory youth officer. They can advise, but they can't dictate.

There simply isn't enough money for the State to provide a blanket youth provision. The role of the voluntary force has now become *crucial* for maintaining a complete range of youth work across the nation. John Egglestone, in his book *Adolescence and Community* noted that it is the voluntary sector which has stood most secure in its boundaries since the war.

Voluntary organisations are held in high esteem; partly because of their contact with powerful élite groups in business, commerce and politics. This has come about largely through drawing representatives of these groups onto management committees. In a Christian context then, it can be useful to have older, successful, Christian business people on the management committee, where they can draw goodwill for the project, from their professional contacts within the community.

For financial reasons, the statutory services cannot provide help outside the twelve to eighteen age group. But these days, young people can be very mature, and set in their ways, before they reach the age of twelve. To throw them onto the streets again once they reach their eighteenth birthday is barbaric; it prevents many young people from being helped into full adulthood in a caring environment.

Of course, the ages have to be broken down into divisions. A five-year-old clearly has different needs from a twenty-five-year-old. At St Paul's, we find it beneficial to run a group for five to seven-year-olds at five o'clock, because that is the time that their fathers come home from work, and it gives the parents the opportunity to sit down quietly together – possibly for the only time during the week. Different activities are needed for different ages, but they are all basically energetic activities, which help the young people to release their energies and pent-up aggression. Eight to twelve-year-olds are basically allowed to run around playing team games, whereas the thirteen to sixteen-year-olds play more competitively.

Young people become more competitive as they reach their mid-teens. It's better for them to have their competitiveness released in an open youth club rather than on the streets, competing to see how many cars they can steal, or how many muggings they can commit.

The senior club, thirteen upwards, tend to play quieter games such as table-tennis, pool and the football machines; though more energetic games like football and volleyball are not uncommon. Once they've worn themselves out playing these games, it becomes easier to sit them down for talks and discussions.

As they get older, we try to use them more in the running of the club. We look for their leadership potential and, if they're not Christians, we try to lead them to a commitment. If they're still hanging around a Christian youth club in their early twenties, then they must like what is being offered.

What does age really matter? If someone is forty-five and still enjoys playing table-tennis, if he's not being offensive to anyone else, what does it matter? (The vicar of a neighbouring parish recently spent an evening showing our members that he could still give them a good game.) It must surely be a good thing if older people show themselves to be interested in the same activities as young people. It simply breaks down the age barriers.

Many people feel that working with youth is strictly for older teenagers, for the youth leader, or for the vicar.

But adults often have many skills and talents that could be used. Adults often have hang-ups about youth work. They feel that they can't help in the church's youth programme because they don't know enough about the theory of youth work, and they feel embarrassed about just going in to play table-tennis. They're probably frightened that they might lose!

I'm eternally grateful for the adults at St Paul's club who drew me back to God after I ran away from him back in 1967. In the next chapter, I'll tell you how that happened,

4

YOUTH EVANGELISM

I couldn't have been more terrified if it had happened in a graveyard in the dead of night.

It was broad daylight and I was walking down Homerton High Street, one autumn morning. I'd just passed Hackney hospital, walking with my head down, when I felt a hand fall on my shoulder. This is it, I thought, the Old Bill's caught up with me at last! The police had been looking for me for the past few days, in connection with a very violent incident which had occurred at an East End pub the previous week.

I nearly jumped out of my skin with shock. Turning around, I fully expected to see a couple of coppers ready to take me in. To my surprise, I found myself face-to-face with John Pearce. I hadn't seen John for quite some time. I was surprised that he even recognised me in my skinhead gear. With my bovver boots, Ben Sherman shirt and Crombie jacket, I looked very different from the way I'd been when I used to go to church, a couple of years previously. It was a week after my eighteenth birthday, and I felt like one of the toughest nuts in town. I doubt that I would have been seen dead talking to a vicar, were it not for my relief that the police hadn't caught me. John had some news for me:

"Clive Skinner's dead. Do you want to come to his funeral?"

"Yeah, sure," I said, a little stunned that the one teacher who could ever get through to me at school should have died so young. He could scarcely have turned thirty.

I managed to avoid the police for the next few days.

John had said that the funeral was to be the following Wednesday and that, if I wanted to go, I should go up to the church the Sunday before, to make the arrangements. It seemed a good idea; I reasoned that the last place that the police would come looking for me was in a church!

It was good to see again the people I'd known at the church three years previously. No one asked me where I'd been, or held any recriminations about me being part of the gang that had chased Ted Longman. I began to relax and, for the first time in days, I stopped worrying about the police being after me.

The funeral itself was the turning point in my life. It was at Oak Hill College, where Clive had been training for the ministry after his stint as an RE teacher. I went up there in the mini-bus from St Paul's, along with the other folk I knew from the church. What really surprised me, during that half-hour drive, was the way everyone reacted to Clive's death. I'd expected everyone to sit in silence, full of their own grief. Instead, everyone seemed happy; they were all singing choruses and praising God for Clive's short ministry! At the service itself it was the same; nothing but praise for God. I wondered if I was in the right place!

There was something very ironical about the situation. There I was, attending a funeral, while the police were looking for me to question me about my involvement in a senseless and bloody beating which – as far as I knew – could easily have led to our victim's death. I was at a friend's funeral at a time when I could easily have been the cause of someone else's funeral. It was that aspect of the situation that really struck me. Perhaps that was why God was able to use it so powerfully.

Filled with pity for the man I'd attacked, I joined in the service, surrendering myself to adoration of God. In the mini-bus, on the way back, I felt so bitterly aware of my own inadequacies, my own guilt, and the total hopelessness of my own existence.

"Are you alright?" asked Angela, John's wife, comforting me.

"No, I'm not!" I said. All the people at the service and all the people in the mini-bus had something that I didn't have, and I wanted it. I wanted their faith – the faith that could turn death into victory. I knelt down in the van, and said a prayer that Angela told me. When I stood up again, I knew that I was a Christian. It was as simple as that.

There had been three deaths: the actual death of Clive Skinner; the death, so I supposed, of the man I'd helped to beat up; and the death of my 'old self' leading to a new life. I'd been broken. I was changed. Being at a funeral had saved me. A fight had taken me away from the Church, and a fight had brought me back.

I felt safe and secure in the company of Christians. I went back to the vicarage for a few days, and I didn't want to leave. I felt that I'd got somewhere; that I'd got somebody; and that I was someone. I knew that I now had access to a better way of life than I'd ever known before.

For one of the first times in my life, I'd shown my feelings; the other Christians at St Paul's seemed to respect me for that. Eventually I told them about the bloodbath for which I'd been partly responsible. There was no condemnation. "You're a Christian now," they said. "Leave the situation to God."

So I did. And when the police finally picked me up for questioning, I told them all about the incident as honestly as I could. I admitted that I'd kicked the victim a few times, but they were more interested in the other gang members – the ones who had attacked with knives and broken bottles. By some miracle, the victim had lived. This wasn't a murder enquiry, as I'd feared.

In the end, I wasn't even called as a witness. The people who were first into the fight, who'd caused the most damage, were all sent to prison. I would have been quite prepared to be sent down myself, but the police had decided that my part in the offence was of too minor a nature even to warrant my being charged.

*

My life had changed, and I'd been evangelised primarily through the power of Christian worship. As John Pearce once said to me "Most young people are looking for something with life and vigour; for something that's fun. Now, if they discover this in a Christian setting, they find it almost irresistible, because it's permanent. If you happen to be at a concert, it's great while you're there, but the feeling goes as soon as you get outside afterwards. When you became a Christian, you were stepping into a para-church group that was already alive. They had a lot of spiritual life and worship of their own."

The kind of group of which I'd become a part was the sort which works most effectively for evangelism even today. All through the 1960s, and 1970s, into the 1980s, we've found that indigenous Christians communicating the gospel to their own culture is far and away the most effective means of bringing eastenders to know the Lord.

The youth-orientated workers at the NIE conference outlined a whole blueprint for urban evangelism, which closely follows the pattern of outreach as I've known it in Hackney. The group concluded that there is a need for

> people who are prepared to persevere in love, pity, attention and practical caring, to identify in suffering, and to sacrifice on behalf of others . . . Others are needed who have a similar background (to people in the inner-city) who are Christians, and who already have some social contact. New Christians, backed up by others, can be bridge people . . . They must be enabled to provide substitute homes and families, presenting models which speak of Christ.

That's what happened with me. I found that provision had been made to enable any young Christians like myself, both to remain in the kingdom, *and* to successfully evangelise our contemporaries from similar backgrounds. The first of these provisions was 'Teenage Bible Studies' to provide solid teaching for young Christian minds. The format that was eventually developed was that of a two-hour session where people would mill around inside the vicarage for an hour or more, listening to records and generally sharing in fellowship, before a formal time of teaching. We had a very traditional Bible study, but in a setting that was happy and free-and-easy. The whole feel was, I suppose, similar to that of a Christian Union – providing an alternative to formal church services – to which young people could relate. Quite a number of chairs and settees seemed to get broken in the early days of that ministry!

The second provision that was needed was 'Sharing Groups' of people prepared to share their lives together, usually with an older Christian present to give advice and guidance. Typically, these groups would meet in private houses, or in the vicarage. But we teenage Christians were never passengers; we would always have a say in determining the way that the church would be run. At one point, more than 50 per cent of St Paul's PCC was under twenty-two.

I attended additional meetings between 4.00 p.m. and 6.00 p.m. on Sundays, to plan special youth services. Although it was a planning meeting, and we always felt that we were achieving something, it was also another opportunity for fellowship. We found that it was especially necessary to provide fellowship, too, over holiday periods – particularly Christmas – when there would otherwise have been a great temptation to go to parties and get drunk, or to sleep with the girlfriend. (Obviously, it was a costly experience, giving up time that one really wanted to spend with one's family, in order to help and protect others, but it was well worth the sacrifice.)

A clear policy of Christian ethics was – and still is – maintained. We totally accept any non-Christian, regardless of their circumstances, and whatever they may have done. But, the moment that they become a Christian, a radical change is expected. We would never lay down the law to anyone outside God's kingdom, or become judgemental with anyone. But once somebody becomes a child of God, it's a different matter – as I'll explain later.

The purpose of these groups – which, I suppose were really home groups or fellowship groups, long before the term came into use, but which were also open to non-Christians – was to affirm the identity and self-worth of young people; to provide security and a sense of belonging. Only when that has been done can we challenge young people to the purpose and meaning in life which comes uniquely through the gospel.

Once we have dispelled ignorance and prejudice about Jesus, and conveyed the significance of Christ's atoning death, we can begin to lead people to pray honestly and realistically, and nurture new disciplines in their own culture. We mustn't brainwash people. We have to give them the Gospel, and disciple them in a manner that is relevant to them within their own culture.

Of course, we've had many problem cases coming into these groups. One young man, who was a little unstable, was very good at playing the guitar – but he was very temperamental and insecure. If he felt, at any point, that anyone disagreed with what he was saying or playing, then he would just get up and leave. On one occasion, he actually smashed up his guitar before storming out of the house. A few weeks later, he would turn up again as though nothing had happened. You have simply to accept that sort of behaviour when dealing with insecure people, in that kind of situation.

On another occasion, there was a spate of petty violence – mainly the non-Christians slashing at each other with sharpened metal combs. Not much damage was ever done, although one or two faces needed minor repairs. It all came to a head with a fight outside the vicarage between two non-Christians who had become regular attenders at an evangelistic home group meeting. Angela Pearce went outside afterwards and brought one of the combatants into the vicarage to bathe his wounds, and the other fighter burst out into tears because he hadn't been brought in to be looked after too!

(Incidentally, the first young man later overdosed on heroin, whilst the second became a Christian. You can never predict how God's gracious spirit will operate.)

Many young people become so attached to these groups, and to the feeling of security and belonging that they generate, that they come to regard the elder members as mother and father figures. I remember, with one particular youth, that this got out of hand. He was asked to come around only on specific days; but the youth began to sleep outside the side door of the vicarage. He was saying, non-verbally, that he'd rather sleep rough to be near Christians, than be tucked up in a warm bed in his own non-Christian household.

Whenever I was in the Pearces' home in those days, I was always impressed by their naturalness – the way that Angela would kiss John in front of other people. Their actions carried strong messages about the way life *should* be – the kind of life that many young eastenders never see in their own families. You could tell that their lifestyle was real; they weren't just putting it on. These days, now I've got my own home, my wife and I hold open home here the way John and Angela used to do. We try our best to follow their example in being totally natural.

It can often be a costly business. John and Angela were regularly burgled; and it's clear that a lot of thieving went on from 'the inside'. On one occasion, twenty pounds was stolen, and John had a shrewd idea who'd taken it. Coincidentally, the suspect – who wasn't a Christian – turned up at the next meeting wearing a brand-new mohair suit that must have set him back, say, all of twenty quid...

Although it didn't take much to put two and two together, nothing was ever said to the culprit. It was more important that he should keep coming to meetings where there remained the possibility of him making a commitment to Jesus, than that he should be punished for a crime that – very probably – had been forced on him by social pressures anyway.

*

After the 'Teenage Bible Studies' and the 'Sharing Groups', the third innovation in our evangelistic programme was the special 'Youth Services'. These were originally held after evensong every Sunday, to cater for young Christians and their non-Christian peers. These people could actually relate to formal evensong – the problem was that the older members of the congregation couldn't relate to the young people! The occasional gossiping during the less-interesting bits of the service caused irritation amongst the more solemn members. Rather than have conflict in the church, it was preferable to give the young people their own tailor-made service afterwards.

These services would generally last about half an hour. They would contain prayer, worship, Bible reading, a two-minute talk, an interview, occasional drama, and always a lot of singing. People would jump up and down and talk through it, but that didn't matter. It was part of their culture to behave like that. It would have been wrong of us to have made them sit still and conform to some middle-class, suburban idea of what church should be like. If they were inattentive, it was because we were not taking the trouble to keep their interest. But when we really gripped them – and there were those moments during every service – they would sit motionless in silent captivation. One of those moments was usually at the end of the service, when we sang the chorus 'Turn Your Eyes Upon Jesus', followed by a time of silence. Often the silence would last for two or three minutes, and we would know that we were really getting through to the uncommitted.

On one occasion, just after one of the non-Christians from the club – a lad called Harvey – had been killed in a car crash, we ran a service with 'death' as the theme. With the fatal accident still on everyone's mind, our presentation of the Gospel message with Christ as the Lord of life who transcended death was particularly striking. I recall the outcry when Johnney Sparks – the Christian giving the talk – said that Harvey had gone to

Hell: "He wasn't a Christian. He didn't want to know."
It wasn't a popular thing to say, but it was the truth, and
I think – eventually – we were respected for being so
honest in our opinions.

Other distinguishing characteristics of the services
were that teaching would be introduced at more than
one point; that there would always be a post-mortem
straight afterwards, to discuss how it had gone, and if it
could be improved for next time; and the bizarre
presence of 'bouncers' in the congregation ready to step
in and keep order if the situation got too out of hand.

These services became less frequent in the late 1970s,
largely because of sudden changes in youth lifestyle –
particularly the punk culture – with which we were
temporarily out of step. But, in 1984, we revived the idea
under the title 'Freedom Gate'. The format was basically
the same, except that we took advantage of more recent
technology by using clips of video to introduce and
illustrate the theme of each service. We seemed to attract
mainly West Indian teenagers at first, but it has
gradually become more multi-racial. Whereas with the
old youth service the problem often was in keeping order,
now the biggest problem is getting the kids to stop
smoking marijuana in the middle of prayers.

The other main difference is that there are virtually *no*
Christians from within their own peer group. There are
youth workers present on a practically one-to-one ratio,
but it's taking time to get the first convert. 'Freedom
Gate' was originally begun at All Souls church, Clapton
Park, (a church in a team ministry with St Paul's) and
attracted ten to fifteen young people. We've now moved
it to the end of a normal club night at St Paul's, and we're
getting fifty to sixty youths. We continue to go out into
the streets, talking to passers-by, handing out tracts and
inviting young people to these services; it's usually the
personal contact which draws people in.

Obviously the main source of contact with people who
come to the service is St Paul's youth club. The club can
be seen as the 'sharp end' of the evangelistic effort. It's

53

always staffed by Christians, and a lot of one-to-one evangelism takes place informally. There's usually an epilogue, but it's not there as a legal formality. We try to make it interesting, but its function is not really to teach. It's there simply to remind the young people that it's a Christian club.

In the past, we've run a late night youth club – from 10.30 p.m. to 1.00 a.m. on a Friday night – that's had an explicitly Christian programme. We'd run it again if we felt that it was still needed. But the bulk of our evangelism *feeds* from the club, rather than taking place within its four walls. I believe that many churches fail to achieve any results in their youth clubs simply because they expect them to be a be-all and an end-all, rather than simply a point of contact with youngsters who can then be drawn in to specific evangelistic programmes.

Young people are not necessarily irreligious. To the contrary, many are on a spiritual quest which can be quite agonising. Milson, in his book *Youth in the Local Church*, suggests that:

> adolescence is often a time when we are looking for a personal philosophy, trying to make sense of the human situation. Most of us are too shy to admit our feelings. But any youth worker who has gained the confidence of a group of young people will find them on occasions discussing, in their own way, profound questions which have teased the philosophers through the ages.

The first secret of inner-city evangelism is to be persistent, not to give up, and not desperately to try something new every couple of weeks – or it soon starts to become like a drowning man clutching at straws. (It's also important to be open with people. "In a good church", says Milson, "the adults do not suppose that they have acquired the complete and absolute truth. Their faith is a river rather than a rock.") We need to be sure that it's Christ we are offering to the young people, and not simply our own idea of what he's like. Remember, we're building the Church of tomorrow –

not preserving our own contribution to yesterday's Church.

In the 1970s, the Church of England's Board of Education commissioned some research into the kind of beliefs that young people actually hold. A group of nineteen to twenty-year-old girls were asked if they would consider going to a church "if it was a happy, jolly place". "It wouldn't be right, would it?" was the reply. Church to them, meant a dull, boring place. There were no instances in the survey, of un-Churched young people being able positively to identify with any liturgical tradition. One particular aspect of the liturgy particularly got their backs up: "There's no discussion, there's just one bloke talking. You just sit there, and you're told. *It's like having ten cups of tea at the same time!*"

Church-going is just not seen as a *normal* adolescent or teenage activity. Something very self-righteous is perceived about going to church. There is a sense of religion being a 'private affair' between each person and God. This, of course, is the opposite of biblical Christianity, with its emphasis on corporate worship.

"The Christian faith is rooted in history", says the *Bewildered but Believing* report:

> this means constantly having to refer back to the life, death and resurrection of Jesus, and to consider the teaching and tradition of the Church over the centuries. As many young adults are particularly interested in the contemporary world, they are bound to feel a tension when looking back to the events surrounding Jesus Christ.

Theology has always recognised itself as having a two-fold function: the first is the preservation of God's eternal truth down the ages, and the second is the interpretation of those eternal truths for each successive generation. The key to fulfilling this second function – and the second secret of successful inner-city evangelism – is to be *relevant*.

In the final two chapters of this book, we shall consider, in detail, how the Church can make itself more relevant – and effective – in its work. For now, it's enough to remember that persistence and relevance are the means by which we can persuade urban young people to unlock their hearts to let in the Saviour. 'Teenage Bible Studies', 'Sharing Groups' and special 'Youth Services' are all tried-and-tested *frameworks* through which we can apply the principles.

5

TRAINING

When young people *do* become Christians in the inner-city, the transformation can be absolutely staggering. Their parents often think they're 'touched' or 'going through a phase'. They find that they have incredible freedom in Christ; it's like a whole new world opening up.

If people have been physically, emotionally and socially deprived for so long, encountering the living God has an impact that those from safe, secure, middle-class homes can never understand. It feels like winning the football pools. It's a new way of life, with purpose and meaning where previously there had been only poverty and despair. For me, I remember, it was like walking through a black hole into a different universe. I felt as though I'd been turned inside out.

New converts at St Paul's are usually nurtured for positions of leadership in the youth club. Oddly enough, no one thought that *I* showed very much leadership potential at the time of my own conversion! One of the other young people in the same Sharing Group as myself, with leadership potential but little involvement in the club itself, was a guy called Jimmy Murphy. Jimmy lived on Kingsmead, a local pre-war council estate which had become run down and known as 'difficult'. At the time, Jimmy was working for a Jewish tailor. I was unhappy in my own job – I must have gone through half a dozen jobs in three or four years – so Jimmy got me a job with him.

Jimmy and I developed an extraordinary rapport. We were both from gang backgrounds, so we hit it off very well. Though our boss was Jewish, he viewed our

Christian faith favourably. Jimmy and I would go into work half an hour early each morning, to pray for our workmates before the working day began. For a short while, we even tried running evangelistic Bible studies together during the lunch hour. We had several regular attenders, but we quickly ran out of ideas. We didn't really have the *training* to reach other people for God.

For a while, Jimmy and I were involved in 'gang smashing'. We would hang around with a vicious gang from the Kingsmead estate. They would be stoned on narcotics for a lot of the time, so Jimmy and I would make sure they didn't hurt themselves. When they came down off their 'high', we'd talk to them about how Jesus could give them a bigger high, permanently. They'd get drunk and get into fights, and we'd be the first to stop it. There would be arguments with bus conductors, and the gang would get thrown off buses; Jimmy and I would not be involved, but we'd get off with them. We identified with the gang – even to the point of standing spreadeagled, hands on a wall, being frisked by the police whenever the gang got stopped. Though I didn't know it at the time, Jimmy and I were effectively filling the roles of detached youth workers in our work with the gang.

We tried to break down the hostilities by liaising with all the various street gangs in Hackney. There had been a lot of tension caused by members of different gangs not knowing each other; they were happy to fight, because all the other gangs seemed to be composed of faceless individuals. But once Jimmy and I started introducing people to members of other gangs, and a personal rapport had been built up, it became a lot harder for gangs to attack each other when many of the members had friends and acquaintances in the other gang. It sounds good in theory, and it worked well in practice. It still does, even today.

Like any other young convert from St Paul's, I was soon back at the youth club, being trained. It didn't have such good equipment as it has now. There was just a snooker table, table-tennis table, a beat-up record player and a small canteen; but a lot of room.

New Christians still become trained simply by joining in and helping to run the club. Anyone with time on his or her hands should feel able to go along and find something – or something could be found for them – which would be beneficial to the church's youth programme. A person doesn't need any particular skill to walk about the club for an hour or two, chatting to young people, and being open to God-given opportunities to speak about faith.

There are, of course, training schemes available for those who wish to become fully-qualified youth workers. A local college of further education will usually be able to provide details of the courses that they run. But, naturally, these approach youth work purely from a secular angle. Many Christians find – as I did! – that their faith is changed or weakened by the constant eroding of Christian values which sometimes takes place on such courses.

A desire to serve is usually more important than formal training – in the beginning, at least – in church-run youth situations. Even introverted people have something to offer. They may be slow or shy, but that doesn't mean that they are not capable. We find that introverts are initially more at home if they are doing something which *brings* people to *them*. I often put them in the coffee-bar or canteen part of the club – or perhaps collecting money on the door – where young people will naturally go to them.

Extroverts need to be careful not to take up too much space. They need to be prepared to *give* people their time, rather than to take the time of others. I find it's important not to be seen as being 'The Leader' – someone on a pedestal, who stands on the door with a big bunch of keys. I don't think it matters whether the young people know who's in charge; they can find out soon enough anyway by asking someone who's been coming longer. Another way is to ask any new youth leaders to go around letting the members know when the facilities are due to close for the day.

Why do volunteer youth workers do their job? Often out of a refreshing need for enjoyment and personal achievement. Surveys suggest that volunteers do not think of the youth work they do as 'work' – they associate work with dissatisfaction and lack of enjoyment – but as more of a social activity, an outlet for relaxation.

Voluntary workers – of say, six months standing – often need to be sent on training courses to spend time considering the different styles of leadership, and to enable them to understand the needs that they will begin to feel – for recognition, self-growth, self-esteem and status – once their initial enthusiasm has worn off. Professional workers like myself need to clarify roles and help the volunteers to develop honest, open, trusting relationships.

Good volunteer leaders at St Paul's are gradually given a certain number of paid hours, financed by the local education authority. More hours are added until they find they can throw in their day job to become a part-time, then a full-time, youth worker on our permanent team. That's roughly the way I got into full-time youth work myself.

For two or three years, back in the early 1970s, I worked as a volunteer in the youth club – and received in-service training – while working for Radio Rentals during the day, to pay the rent! My parents moved out of Homerton to a different part of Hackney, called Hoxton, but I kept returning to St Paul's youth club, where I believed that the Lord wanted me to be. The commuting was punishing, and eventually I moved into a house in Hackney, as a member of the Community of the Word of God – a group of Christians living together. They supported me so that I could become a youth worker on a full-time basis.

My calling actually to *lead* the project came in a way that resembled something in a story-book. About six or seven of the potential leaders, myself included, went down to a church near the East India Dock Road for an evening of prayer and discussion to decide who would take charge of the youth work. We sat around in a circle and each said why they felt they were suitable, or otherwise, to be the new leader. Then John Pearce, who was leading our discussion, said, "I want each of you to go away into separate rooms to think and pray about who should be the leader. In two hours' time, I'll call you together and give each of you a piece of paper. Then I want you each to write down the name of the person whom you think is God's choice."

John wanted to be sure that we picked God's man for the job, so he put a fleece before the Lord; he wanted the seven of us to come to a unanimous decision. Well, after an hour and a half of praying, I started getting very worried. I was becoming more and more convinced that, when the time came, I should write down my *own* name on the paper! Half an hour later, I trooped out and did just that. I felt a right fool. John collected the papers together and began to turn them over, one at a time. I was convinced that six of the seven would have someone else's name on them and that, when mine came up, everyone would look at me and laugh at me for voting for myself. I didn't dare look.

"Right," said John, "We've got a unanimous choice. You're our new youth leader, Pete!"

I really didn't feel that I could do the job. In fact, I'd said so before we'd each gone off to pray; and I certainly hadn't done it out of modesty. I told the others that they would all have to support me and back me up.

Two years later, it seemed right that I should become a qualified, professional worker, so – with the backing of the church – I began a two-year course at the YMCA national college, in North London. I'd hoped to continue working at St Paul's club during the evenings, but the college made it clear that – for the first year at least – this wasn't on.

Since YMCA stands for Young Men's *Christian*

Association, I'd naïvely expected to be taught an evangelical approach to youth work; but I soon discovered my mistake. There was little real Christian life at the college – most Christians that I met seemed to be liberals – so it was like being in a spiritual wilderness.

On the more positive side, I learned a great deal about how to analyse group situations. The psychology of human interactions can be fascinating. Did you know, for example, just how many reasons there can be for belonging to a particular group? We were asked our reasons for being on the course, as members of our particular student group. Amongst the twenty-two reasons that we came up with were: to seek knowledge; to become qualified; to gain experience; to impress others; for status; for security of profession; to ease our social consciences; and to prove that we are serious about doing youth work.

If a person were to join a football team, or a band, what would his motives be? Or for joining a group of people going down to a pub? Try these reasons: to meet people; to share experiences; to meet the opposite sex; to loosen tensions; for a change of environment; for enjoyment; for relaxation; or for fear of being left out. All of them, incidentally, would be good reasons for deciding to join a youth club. When anyone is asked their reasons for doing anything, there are usually at least three 'types' of reason: the one they actually give; the reason they keep to themselves; and the subconscious reason, of which they may not even be aware.

This sort of thinking may seem, on the surface, to be just a load of useless, intellectual claptrap. But it is very important to anyone working professionally with youth to be aware of what is *really* happening in a group situation, and what the members are *really* expecting to get out of being there. If you don't – or can't – do that, then you're going to be lumbered with a lot of discontented teenagers.

An adolescent boy may join other adolescents because he sees a lot of what is in him, in them. But his subconscious reason may be that he's after one of the girls with whom they hang around. Nothing is pure and simple, we were taught. Even in easily explainable situations, there may be some ulterior motive.

Often people need pushing into something that they might be good at. "Roger, I think you would be very good at refereeing the football match," I might say to someone in our club. "You must be joking," could be the reply, but Roger might really be saying, "Do you really want me to do it? Do you think that I would be capable?" Depending on our relationship, I could tell whether he was asking me to push it even more, whether he truly did want to do it and was hesitant about coming forward, or if he honestly did mean "No! Absolutely not." It's important to beware of pat answers.

Situational needs are another important consideration. What are situational needs? Here's an example from my college notes:

> Some women wanted to make eiderdowns, so a local youth worker got them together during the day, and let them use the club premises. The tables were placed in a circle and the women started to work. But they were so far apart that, if the women wanted to talk, they had to shout. In the end, they didn't speak, and the group quickly folded. Why? Probably because, although they wanted to make eiderdowns, they were lonely or bored during the day. They wanted to talk and have companionship. Those were the real needs in the situation.

You can learn a lot about people's motives simply through observation. The first duty of love is to watch and listen; to learn more about people in order to discover their real needs. In club situations, it's often helpful – especially if you're new to a particular club – to write down notes each evening. The recording of observations helps to concentrate them in the mind. The particular observations made about people may not seem interesting or important to you, but they're probably important to *them*.

I've still got the notes of my observations at a club in Thanet, where I served a placement as part of my training. They're very revealing:

11 November 1974. Felt scrutinised by everybody. Difficult to relax. Had to go and speak to people, no one came to me. One boy came in with rubbers on that belonged to the club, so the Senior Youth Worker took them off him. [Boy did I feel out of place!]

14 November 1974. Much more at ease. I collected the subscriptions and ran the canteen. Got to know some of the kids. Dido came in from Hillingdon. Played snooker with Gary, who had been coming here for over a year. The girls seem to stick together, and follow each other around. A few of the stronger boys did some weightlifting. [Here, I was starting to remember faces and names, and was able to follow some of the social behaviour of the club.]

24 November 1974. Played table-tennis with Ian. I noticed at first that he was playing me very vigorously. He won the first game, and was leading in the second, when he began to relax and not try so hard. In the third game, it was as if he wasn't bothered. [This is an interesting observation of Ian's motives. Though his apparent motivation was to win, when he let his guard down, it became obvious that really he only wanted my company and wasn't concerned about the game.]

A lot of the theories that I was taught at college, I already knew instinctively, but I never knew how or why certain techniques worked. My training gave me a thorough grasp of the rationale behind the various approaches to situations that commonly occur in youth work. But the training did something else too. It made me doubt my faith. The steady diet of humanist-based teaching gave me more confidence in myself as a person, but it destroyed my initiative – my gut feeling – approach to relating to young people, and it left me puzzled as to where God fitted into youth work.

I later discovered that *many* youth workers have difficulty in putting the 'gut feeling' they get in work situations into objective terms. They may be late for an important meeting because they *felt* they ought to stay a while longer with a particular group of kids; but it's difficult to explain that to a management committee. Emotions are of vital importance in youth work – to a greater extent than is generally realised.

When we workers express our feelings, they often unintentionally come out in a negative way. There is a need for 'gut feelings' to be more fully understood and then communicated more positively. Many youth workers find it difficult to express their problems. There is a fear of exposing personal weakness through expressing feelings; and workers need to be more sensitive, tactful and responsible, in expressing their 'gut feelings'.

As workers we need to be able to communicate what our work is about, and to know what questions to ask the young people with whom we work in order to be able to help them. It is essential that we recognise the messages that other people give out, and are able to use them positively. A youth worker needs to be able to establish his/her own personal framework with which to relate to other people; to receive support; and to help the young people with whom he/she works.

Youth work is an extraordinarily diverse field of activities. It seems unlikely that there will ever be an agreed, tidy definition of its scope and purposes. That, of course, makes it a very difficult field in which to train others. Several Christian organisations, such as British Youth For Christ (BYFC) and Frontier Youth Trust (FYT) run courses, and I recently saw an advert in *Buzz* magazine for a course. It's good that Christians are now heavily involved in the training of youth workers. But in the early seventies, when I was heading towards a crisis – with my intuitive Christian approach to youth work apparently at odds with the 'proper' way of doing things – I felt alone.

"Isolations. Unclear aims. Confused feelings. Difficult communications. These are some of the difficulties faced by many workers in the community and, perhaps more than most, by detached youth workers," says Warren Redman, in his pamphlet *Guidelines to Finding Your Own Support*. If only someone had told me that when I was feeling so unsure of myself. Warren suggests several ways in which youth workers can get support: sharing mutual support with a second worker; working in a threesome; writing down your feelings quickly after something happens; recording your feelings and reactions to situations on tape, and then playing them back; using an outside consultant – possibly a member of the management committee; forming a 'task group' of perhaps half a dozen local youth workers, who meet to discuss common needs in their work; and forming a 'tutorial group', similar to a 'task group', but with an outside counsellor to direct discussions.

I just wish that someone had come along with some suggestions when I was feeling such isolation as a youth worker during my in-course placement at Ellesmere Port...

6

DETACHED YOUTH WORK

"Oh aye! A cockney, are you?" said the burly-looking man, leering at me. In his forties, he must have been; and built like a heavyweight wrestler.

I'd been heading back to Ellesmere Port one night. I had borrowed a van to visit a group of local young people – the Sutton group, they were called – for whom I'd tried to set up a youth group in an old church hall. Coming back, I'd seen the burly man at the side of the road, thumbing a lift.

Well, he didn't really qualify as a young person, but since my full title is Youth and *Community* Worker, I thought that I'd help this particular member of the community by giving him a lift to his destination. But I soon began to wish that I hadn't bothered!

"I don't like cockneys," he said.

One quickly becomes used to dealing with all manner of odd situations as a youth worker, but this was a new one on me. The guy smelt like a brewery. I was hoping that he wouldn't try anything while we were moving that would make me lose control of the vehicle.

"I live around *there*," he said in his scouse accent, gesturing to a particular housing estate that we were fast approaching.

"Right, I'll drop you off, mate," I volunteered, hoping that I could get him out of the van without him taking a swipe at me. The tone of his voice was changing all the time, getting heavier and heavier, as he described all the cockneys he'd ever known and what they'd done to him.

"Is it here then, mate, that you live?" I asked as we approached what seemed to me to be a good dropping-off point. He slurred some remark to the affirmative, and I brought the van to a halt – with my feet on the clutch and foot brake.

"Just pull back the handle," I said, gesturing towards the door. He opened it and placed one foot on the pavement outside. He was still calling cockneys by all the rude names that he could think of, probably hoping that I'd react violently so that he'd have an excuse to clunk me. I reacted alright, but not in the way that he'd expected.

I'd noticed that, though he was still partly in the van, most of his weight was transferred to the foot on the ground outside. The van was still in first gear and, with practised ease I transferred my right foot to the accelerator, while letting out the clutch. With a roar, the van took off – throwing my assailant clear, to sprawl in a heap by the side of the road.

After that, I was *very* careful to whom I gave a lift!

It wasn't a very Christian thing for me to have done, but that summed up my attitude towards my work at the time. In Ellesmere Port, I just got on with my job of relating to young people; but I know now that a lot of what I did was wrong, and now I regret it.

One particular incident really sums it up for me. Though I spent some time working in a secular youth club, I was also involved as a detached youth worker with another group. I'd met them in the street, and befriended them. I attached myself to them and went everywhere that they went. One evening, they'd arranged to take a train into Liverpool to see the band Status Quo at the Liverpool Empire. Expecting this to be a costly trip, I took plenty of cash with me. In the end, it turned out that I didn't need any of it.

Firstly, the kids timed their arrival at the station so that the train was just pulling out. "We'll pay at the other end," they said, rushing past the ticket barrier. Once aboard, they avoided an inspector by moving down the train ahead of him and – when the train pulled into a station – alighting and running along the platform to board the train again behind him! At the ticket barrier at the other end, they blended with the crowd and pushed past the ticket collector before he realised what was going on.

When we arrived at the concert, I began to think that they'd reformed when the first gang member went up to buy a ticket. But he was the only one who paid. Once inside, he waited till the band came on stage and the security men were distracted by the audience rushing to the front, then he let the rest of us in through the fire exit!

I was very naïve. I mistakenly thought that being a detached worker with a gang meant doing what they did, in order to be accepted as part of the group. But detached work isn't that at all. Many detached workers make the mistake of thinking that, once they've managed to identify with the kids, they can somehow change them. But what can easily happen is that the worker loses direction and winds up as violent and lawless as those that he is trying to help.

For me, it was a very painful learning experience. Where was my work? I'd earned the lads' trust, by doing what they did in breaking the law. But I wasn't *working* with them. What I should have done was to say, "Look, you've made space for me in the group. You're happy for me to come along, so you'll have to wait for me while I buy a ticket for myself. I'm going to express the *power* that you've let me have in your lives."

Eventually, I started to do that. Wherever we went, I'd pay for myself while they did their fare evasion. "You're daft," I'd tell them. "You've all got police convictions. Is it worth being sent to jail for the sake of a few bob?" My attitude eventually came across to them, and the time came when – one by one – they began to say "Okay Pete, I'll pay too."

Sadly, changing the young people's attitude towards fare evasion was my only success. Though I still had standards for myself, I'd convinced myself that those standards didn't matter – that I mustn't let them come between me and the young people with whom I was working. At Ellesmere Port, the kids I worked with all smoked dope; so I joined them to be part of the group. I thought I'd be accepted if I got drunk with them – so I got drunk. I thought I'd be accepted if I fell over with them – so I fell over. In the end, there was nothing to distinguish me from the group with which I was supposedly working.

During my time at college, in addition to the three-month placement at Ellesmere Port, I also undertook field work in Israel. The course was very challenging. Afterwards, it took me a long spell at Taizé – a religious community in the south of France – to sort myself out again. Even then, the process wasn't complete. Taizé showed me that I could be a Christian in the world, or so I thought at the time. Unfortunately, rather than becoming in-tune with God, I became in-tune with myself. I reasoned everything out for myself, and never stopped to think, "what would Jesus have done in this situation?" When I returned to Hackney – as a detached youth worker – my training had made me a very different person from the old Pete Stow who used to help out at the old, beat-up St Paul's club, before I went to college.

I think the only reason that I returned to Hackney was because I needed some security. I'd felt secure at college, but now, with my former classmates dispersed around the country, I was alone once more. John Pearce and I had discussions with the local statutory youth officer and worked out a full-time post for me back at St Paul's. Although I served two nights per week at the youth club, my main task for the other three nights and during the day, was to get out into the streets and seek out the kids as they hung around on street corners and in shop doorways. I was to relate to their needs on the street in the same way that a club worker related to youth in a club environment; but it was hard that way, due to the lack of support. I had to go boldly where no youth worker had gone before!

My objective, when I first took on the job, was to find some young non-Christians. By that time, in 1976, the St Paul's club seemed to be attracting mostly Christian young people, It seemed to have got itself, temporarily, into a holy huddle. There were still street gangs around, but they weren't affecting us. More importantly, *we* weren't affecting *them*. My job was to go out and find where they had got to!

There must be some people who, if they could observe a detached worker in his first month on a new patch, might conclude that it's the easiest job in the world. To all intents and purposes, all the youth worker appears to do is to wander around the streets all day, trying to find out where the kids go, and where the gangs gather.

But what is *really* happening is that the worker is studying the social patterns of an area. What sort of homes do people have? What kind of shopping facilities are available? How do people move about? People in flats usually have some sort of communal hall or lobby, which is a focus of interest. Often, it can be a stairwell where people gather. But for people in houses, the centre of interest might be a school or shopping centre. The worker examines how the young people meet their social needs – be it through pubs, clubs, cinemas, back alleys or launderettes.

Upon finding a gang, or a lone kid, it's no use going up and telling them about the Gospel straight out, because the worker would be written off as a nutter. The only communication that can take place, at first, is to simply nod an acknowledgment at the young people. As the days go by, that nod may extend to "Hello", or "Nice day", until the time is right to begin a conversation. To try to go too fast is to presume on a relationship that has not yet been formed.

I found it useful, with groups, to work out who were the leaders, and to concentrate on being their friend, first and foremost. I remember with one gang, the leader was interested in football – the gang were playing a game – so I went up to him and said "Can I play?" After the game, we went to the pub and chatted. The initial contact had

71

been made. After weeks, or months, of slow work, it became possible to say to the young people, "Look, other people may think you're not acceptable, but you're not unacceptable to me. *You* don't have to adapt; *I* will adapt. I will try to bridge the gaps."

The purpose of detached, or outreach, youth work is not to try to persuade the young people to go to clubs. There are many young people who don't like youth clubs; it just isn't their scene because they are too individual to fit in. Oh sure, there are occasions when young people really *do* want to belong to a club, but have never been given the opportunity; but, for the most part, detached work involves finding out their dreams and aspirations, and striving with them to make them become realities. In Ellesmere Port, I'd met a gang who'd wanted to form a motor-bike club, and I'd helped them to do so. In Hackney, I found that a lot of young people's aspirations were often very low. People can fall into the trap of thinking about little more than how to live from one day to the next. Tomorrow is another day – a new beginning.

A club worker has young people come to him, but the detached worker has to go to them. He or she has to gain their trust and to become recognised as a part of the group. Not just one group, either. After a few months, I was relieved of any responsibilities in St Paul's club, so that I could devote myself fully to the detached work, and I soon had a choice of groups with whom I could spend my time. I knew all their haunts, the pubs where they drank, and the streets where they lived. If there was a group that began to feel I was in their way, then I'd stop working with them, and move to another group. It can be very positive for a group to say "That's it. There's nothing more that you can do for us. On your way!" The object of any piece of detached work is to talk, discuss and explore oneself into redundancy.

Take, for example, the first gang with which I worked.

I met them on the street at first, but quickly found out which pub they frequented – it was The Adam and Eve. They'd all sit around with their pints of lager, saying how they were hard done by. "If I knew then what I know now," they'd all say. They were only seventeen or eighteen years old, but they were talking like old men. Many of them were hanging onto the past, so I had to teach them how to live for the present. I found that it was largely confidence they lacked, so I often had to let them lean on me for moral support, until they were able to stand up for themselves.

I had some quite extraordinary times with the gang. I particularly recall one of the gang members named Adrian. Adrian was disgusting! We always knew that he was so skint that he'd do anything for money, but I never thought he'd resort to the antics he got up to one night in The British Oak. One of the other gang members poured together the dregs from a dozen different beer glasses, added a few empty crisp and nut packets – along with a liberal sprinkling of cigarette ash – and told Adrian that he could have a fiver if he drank it. It made me feel sick to see him guzzling it down. But the guy who had taunted him into doing it had no intention of paying; it was all a joke. A laugh – nothing more.

And it was a joke too, when we all ran out and decided to have a race down the street outside. But the laughing stopped when we all collided with an iron bar that stretched out knee-high across our path! As we limped home nursing our bruises, there was a real comradeship. We felt like troops that had been wounded in action together.

On another occasion, the gang decided to go 'skinny dipping' – swimming in the nude – in the nearby River Lea, at midnight! If I'd declined to join them, I would have lost the respect of the group – and they'd have thrown me in anyway – so I stripped off and jumped in. But, oh boy, was that water cold!

After I'd won the gang's confidence, I could begin to help them to let go of the hurts and disappointments of the past. Gradually, they all discovered new interests that took them away from the gang. There was, for instance, one guy who wanted to be a footballer. He was good, so I helped him to find a team that would take him on. I nurtured the confidence of each of them in turn, to help them to break with the past and find something fresh that was worth living for. Eventually, the gang was reduced to a small handful who met spasmodically, when there had once been a few dozen who met every night. My job with that particular group had been done.

Detached work – for me – meant always being available. The young people knew where I lived, and they'd come around whenever they had a problem that they wanted to discuss with me. Often I'd sit up with them half the night trying to help them to resolve their difficulties. There are some people who think that a detached worker should not live in the area where he works; that he – or she – should go off on a Friday night, and not return until the Monday morning. But the problems, I always found, would occur over the weekend. That was always the time when the young people would get drunk, stoned, or into a fight, and need patching up. They couldn't go home in that condition, or their parents would throw them out. I'd phone up anxious parents and explain that their little Jimmy was okay and would be stopping at my flat for the night. I found that this type of 'emergency work' over the weekend was a perfect way to break down barriers with the young people.

"Detached work is the cutting edge of youth work," says my colleague Pete Ellem. "On the street, it's harsher than in a club. It's life in the raw. It's the place where pain is going to be dealt out; often between people who call each other friends, but who aren't always good friends to each other at all."

Peter thinks of himself as being like an absorbent sponge, taking in all the pain as kids knock their feelings off against their detached worker. Our feeling is that it's better for the young people to shout and swear at us, to

74

let out their repressed tension in our vicinity – because we can take it – rather than get into fights or go mugging old ladies. In fairness though, there are some detached workers who find it better to share their feelings when they're shouted at by the kids. "If someone upsets me, then I have to tell them that they've upset me," says Sue Gibbson. "One group in particular used to upset me through their attitude to women. The group called their women 'veggies'; it's short for vegetables. I'm a person with feelings, and I have to share them." There is a balance that needs to be struck between being seen to be reliable and dependable, and being seen to be honest with young people.

Anyone who is thinking of doing some unpaid detached work for their own church may find that it's best to take a friend with them for the first few times, not just for safety reasons, but for support and confidence. Women in particular may find this useful when there are kerb-crawlers about. (But male workers can have problems from the opposite sex too, with girls who want to establish something more than a platonic relationship.) Certainly no more than two people should go together, or it looks too threatening. Personally, I've never felt in any real physical danger during my time as a detached worker. There is often protection against any gang member who wants to take a swipe at a youth worker, from the other gang members who see the worker as being their friend.

It's quite important for a detached worker to keep notes. For a start, it's a lot easier to remember the names of the people that you meet if they're written down. But noting down incidents can be helpful, too. Pete Ellem once told me how, while he was working on a project to convert a disused launderette into a 'den' for the local lads, a guy called Richard said how he would like to have his name put forward for the election of leaders for the scheme. Pete thought that Richard had only mentioned this in passing, as a casual fancy, and was not really serious. But, a couple of weeks later, Richard started behaving strangely towards him. It took a long time for Pete to realise that Richard had actually meant "Please put my name down." He wanted recognition, but only knew how to ask for it in a round-about way. If Pete had noted down Richard's original comment, even though it didn't seem important at the time, it might have helped him understand Richard's strange behaviour, when reviewing his notes.

Detached youth work can be performed effectively in rural areas, as well as in the inner-city, though the problems there are often very different. Sue recalls her placement in a Cambridgeshire village where the main problem lay not with deprivation, violence or drug abuse, but from thirteen and fourteen-year-olds getting drunk. On another placement, at a tranquil seaside resort, the problem stemmed from kids riding their bikes up and down the promenade seeing how close they could ride to the pensioners without knocking them over! But, in the inner-city, detached work is not so much a possibility as a necessity.

In a club situation, young people come for the facilities that are on offer; but in detached work, they are more interested in what the *worker* has to offer. If part of the 'package' which the worker has to offer is his or her Christian faith, then it is quite easy to share that naturally. Once I have established a real relationship with a young person, they usually want to know more about my faith. Many Christian detached workers don't mention their faith until they're asked; but, for me, one of the first steps I took when meeting a group or individual, was to make it clear that I was a Christian. Dressed in denim, I probably didn't conform to their preconceptions of how a church-goer should appear, so there was little danger of them immediately dismissing me as a do-gooder.

"How effective was my approach?" I asked Nick Simpson, who used to be a member of one of the gangs with which I worked: "You used to come straight out

76

and say 'I'm a Christian, and I love Jesus!' and I used to think, 'Bloody hell! He's a bit of a weirdo!' I think it was Pete the Person that I related to first. The fact that you were a Christian didn't seem to matter to us. The fact that you cared for us, and demonstrated that by your attitude and by the way you spent time with us, were the important things. It was once we got to know you that we started asking why you did the things you did."

I guess that I must have really put the Gospel across to Nick eventually, because he became a Christian and he's now one of my fellow workers at St Paul's club.

Crises always seem to throw up opportunities to witness for Christ. Once, Pete Ellem was sitting with a lad who was about to appear in the Crown Court on a serious charge. The guy was reading Psalms, and really seemed to identify with the predicament of the psalmist. Pete was able to say, "If God can help you with this, then he can help you all the time." I often say to people, when they're going to court, that I will pray for them. I tell them that they're never alone and that – whether they believe it or not – God *will* be there with them.

A detached worker usually works with little supervision. These days, with more than one detached worker on the team, regular weekly staff meetings keep the team in touch with one another. But, during *my* time as a detached worker, I was working on my own with only occasional management committee meetings to which to report. Most management committees need to be 'drawn out' before they begin to see the real potential of the mission that the worker is performing. A worker needs approval. He needs to feel a sense of the committee being behind him and really supporting him. It's a rare committee that can do that fully.

When I was a detached worker, I began to feel lonely and unsupported. I really needed a second worker to join the project alongside me, but the necessary financial support couldn't be found. I became more and more disillusioned, and found myself racing towards a crisis point . . .

7

THE PRESSURES

I felt lost. I just didn't know who I was. It had reached the stage where I couldn't relate to evangelical Christians any longer. I'd pop into the club and they'd ask me to do an epilogue, but I just didn't know how to do it any more. John Pearce had to sign a form saying that my first year – my probationary year – as a youth worker was satisfactory. He didn't want to do it, because I'd been so bad! In the end, he must have realised that it was really my Christian commitment to the work that had plummeted and that, as pure youth work, my performance was adequate.

When I arrived home from work, and lay on my bed at night, I felt isolated and alone. All the peace with God that I'd had before going to college had evaporated. I'd started smoking dope again, on a regular basis, but I was hiding it from the other Christians on the staff team. At team meetings, John would ask me questions, but I wouldn't answer. "I'm just not interested," I'd say. The job was all consuming, and every waking hour was given over to it. My work had replaced God in my life. I know that the training I received from college was largely responsible but, looking back, I think that the lack of real support from others was the overriding factor. Perhaps if I'd had the second worker that I'd wanted, to work alongside me, the situation might have developed differently. As it was, I'd simply backslid into my old pre-Christian ways.

It was the issue of the second worker that eventually brought the situation to a head. I'd done a lot of work to establish the need; statistics had been gathered, letters had been written and the relevant books had been consulted. I'd convinced myself that I could win my case to fund a second worker from the Inner London Education Authority (ILEA), but the local youth officer curtly dismissed it: "There's no way that you're going to get another worker." I felt betrayed. My first reaction was to write out my resignation from St Paul's youth project, and slip it through John's door. I'd already thrown God out of my life, and now I was ridding myself of the restriction of His Church.

Finding a new job wasn't difficult. George, my flatmate, worked full-time on a local adventure playground. I knew all the other workers, along with the GLC officer who ran the playground. Getting a part-time job there required only a formality. The next step was to find a flat of my own, where I could spend time by myself.

I look back on that time as my introverted period. Like a recluse, I'd sit round the house all day. Most of my time was spent either deep in thought – trying to work out my own identity – or in reading existentialist books, such as the novels of Hermann Hesse. Hesse is a very mystical writer and I found that I could identify with many of his characters; particularly the taut, introverted main character in *Steppenwolf*. Like a fifties beat-poet, or a sixties hippy, the Pete Stow of the late seventies was on a quest for self-knowledge.

It was quite an extraordinary thing for a native eastender to do, but it stemmed, I suppose, from the training that I'd received at college. They used to tell me at college that the human brain contains millions of brain cells. Sure, they die off – but they're soon replaced. "There's no reason why any of you can't be brilliant," they'd say. Their message was that 'Man is Great.' Whereas before when I had a problem, I'd always go and pray about it, now I thought, "Why bother to pray about it, when I've got to think it out in the end anyway? If God has given me a brain, why don't I just use it?" I kept cancelling God out of my life, whenever I began to fear that he was getting back in again.

In practical terms, I hurt a lot of Christians by being verbally aggressive when they wanted me to go to church. Even at college, I'd behaved thoughtlessly towards my fellow students. One of the other students had been a very loud-mouthed, aggressive girl who would constantly harangue everyone on feminist issues. Instead of respecting her views, I told her in no uncertain terms that she was too forward in her views. (Mind you, I soon wished that I hadn't bothered. She gave me a tongue-lashing in return. It was obvious that she'd thought out her arguments more thoroughly than myself. She opened up a whole vista of sexism to me, with such eloquence that I finished up agreeing with her!)

College had broken down all my assumptions, and put nothing in their place. Losing sight of God and looking inwards upon myself was claustrophobic. I'd become an existentialist, but it brought me no satisfaction. The only answer that seemed to beckon, like a candle-glow at the end of a long dark tunnel, was *suicide*! I felt that I wanted to wander off somewhere, like some romantic mystic, and lie down and die. That's how low I'd become. The loneliness was unbearable. I felt like a character out of Orwell or Huxley – two other authors in whose work I was engrossed.

The nineteenth-century writer Stephen Crane summed up the pessimism that I felt when he wrote: "If I should cast off this tattered coat, and go free into the mighty sky; if I should find nothing there but a vast blue, echoless, ignorant – what then?" What a desperate person I'd become. Lost to me was the majesty of a universe vibrant with God's being. My outlook was very different from that of the psalmist who gazed heavenward and wrote:

> When I look up into the sky which you have made, at the moon and the stars which you set in their places – what is man that you think of him; mere man that you care for him? Yet you made him inferior only to yourself; you crowned him with glory and honour. (Ps. 8: 3-5 GNB)

When I reached my lowest ebb, it began to dawn on me that suicide was no answer at all. The problem wasn't that I wanted to finish myself off, but that I wanted to sort myself out. It was when I reached that point that the tide began to turn. Facing my own personal Gethsemane, I heard – in my mind – God saying: "Here is my hand. I will help you." I was able to say truthfully, "Yes God, I want to take your hand. I want you, God. It was when I turned away from you that everything started to go wrong." I physically dropped to my knees, and held out my arms, praying that God would help me. I felt as though I was being pulled up from the bottom of a deep, dark well. For the first time in months, I felt real peace. It felt as though God were putting back together the jigsaw puzzle that my life had become.

That evening, at about six o'clock, I went out and phoned up John Pearce. He's one of those people who it's practically impossible to get hold of during an evening; he's always booked up for five or six weeks in advance. "John, I've got to talk to you. There's something that I must tell you," I said. I'd fully expected him to say that he wouldn't be able to find time to meet me for at least a fortnight. But, instead, he said, "It's funny that you should phone, Peter, I've just had another call cancelling a meeting that I was supposed to have attended this evening. I can see you straight away."

When we met, and I explained what had happened to me, we were both very close to tears. I felt really sorry that I'd hurt John so much. He was very forgiving, and helpful in drawing me back into the fellowship again. I began attending Sunday services and Bible studies again. Gradually, I started going back to the youth club; at first just once each week, then more often, until I was in there every night that it was open. That was at the end of 1978. I gave up my job at the adventure playground the following summer, and took over the youth club again. I've never looked back!

As a result of my experiences, my faith has been strengthened. It's no longer a blind faith, but a reasoning

81

faith. I quickly realised, not how God fitted in with what I'd learned at college, but how the academic teaching fitted in with the greater glory of God's revelation. The teaching had to be held up to the light of God's truth. If it conformed, then it was acceptable and could be used safely. But if it was in conflict, then it had to be treated with the gravest suspicion.

Sadly, it is not an uncommon occurrence for inner-city Christians – particularly those who work alone – to backslide and not all are as lucky as myself, in being able to re-establish themselves in the faith. Take Fred, for example. Fred was an extraordinarily together young man, whom the other lads all regarded as an intellectual. "He's a bit of a thinker," they'd all say. When Fred became a Christian, he was an unemployed drug-addict. Within weeks of his conversion, he'd come off drugs and found himself a job. Fred wanted to go back to his old mates, to witness to them about what God had done in his life. He wanted them to become followers of Christ, as he had become. Gradually, he began to spend more and more time with them. Just as a good detached worker would do, he identified with them – going everywhere they went, and doing whatever they did. He was with them more than he was with the other Christians and, consequently, he was cut off from real fellowship and support. Slipping further away from God, he began to score drugs again; cannabis, LSD and heroin. Now he's in the psychiatric ward at Hackney hospital, a tragic story.

My time away from Hackney was the beginning of my downfall. To me, the best form of training that a youth worker can have is in-service training. These days, all our workers are trained by actually doing the job – under my supervision – and discussing their performance with me afterwards, so they never have to take on the burden of working alone. We often send workers to night school, or away on courses, but they're never subjected to intensive doses of godless learning without having the opportunity to see how the academic work actually helps in a practical youth club situation. And there are always other Christians around, with whom they can discuss any attacks on their faith that might come from exposure to secular ideas. (Recently, I've been leading a course myself, on behalf of ILEA. It's just a basic four-week induction course, for new youth workers; but at least I can ensure that it's presented without a humanist bias!)

A second pressure on an inner-city youth worker (or vicar, for that matter) comes from a lack of time for him or herself. It's easy to fall into the trap, as I did, of always being available for twenty-four hours of the day. The feeling of constantly being on duty makes relaxation difficult. It's too easy to become so run-down that both the job and the worker's personal life suffer. Sue Gibbson believes that it is fatal to become work-orientated. Life becomes distorted, and the worker loses a lot of his/her own personality. "At the end of the day, the worker has far less to give the young people than if they'd physically detached themselves and done something else for relaxation. When I was living close to the club where I worked", Sue says, "kids were coming around at nine o'clock in the morning and eleven o'clock at night. I was having fits in the kitchen, throwing crockery about because I couldn't take it any more." Self-discipline is needed to be able to say, genuine emergencies with-standing: "This is my afternoon off. Whoever knocks on my door, for whatever reason, they're not coming in. This is my time, for myself."

It seems to me that open youth work has never been taken *seriously* by many churches. That, sadly, is why their youth leaders often seem to be making no progress. They need real encouragement and support in their work, if they are to stand firm against the pressures upon them. In addition to the pressures that I've just mentioned, there is a third source of pressure, which divides itself into several sub-categories. There are the problems which workers have to face, which stem from the everyday work of the club or youth project.

One of my biggest headaches is often over administration. It's got to be done, but it usually takes up a lot of valuable time that could better be given over to face-to-face work with the club members. I don't have a secretary because ILEA won't pay for one, and as a project we can't afford one. My wife does a lot of typing for me, and generally keeps me in order. But I'm not a natural administrator, and it's a pressure that I can do without.

A problem for many clubs, is finding suitable accommodation. It's not a good idea, we found, to run a youth club in the same room or rooms that are used for more restrained activities such as Bible studies, Mothers' Union meetings and PCC meetings. The amenities need to be very robust. It's no good giving young people a room where they have to 'behave themselves', 'not make a mess', 'not write on the walls', and 'clean up after themselves'. We found, and still find, that a room or hall with a wooden floor (now partly carpeted), lighting, heating and bright wall decoration, will suffice.

Pool tables, football machines and video-games machines have been gradually added to the club over the years. Yes, it was expensive, but we found that many of the items could be hired. We looked in the Yellow Pages, and let our fingers do the walking!

Many churches ask, "But what will happen if our hired pool table gets damaged?" That's the wrong question. Ask instead, "What will we do *when* our pool table gets damaged." That way, if the table survives – as it probably will – it will come as a pleasant surprise. (And if the reader thinks that St Paul's youth club has more money than sense, I should point out that it's supported by a very poor and hard pressed church. But to try to run our youth facilities in a more penny-pinching manner would be like trying to make an omelette without breaking eggs.)

We've found that the best way to avoid damage to the equipment is to establish a rapport with the users so that they see the games equipment as being *theirs*. They are much less likely to damage something they see as belonging to *them*, than they are of damaging something that belongs to someone else.

One way to do this, is to start up operations with just the premises, and a ball to kick around (remembering, of course, to ensure that there is wire meshing over the windows.) Then suggest, "Wouldn't it be nice if we had a pool table? How are we going to get one? Shall we start subscriptions?" If the young people contribute even a small amount towards it, they will have much more respect for the property.

Recently, our club's stereo system was stolen. I contacted the police, but they held out little hope of its recovery. I mentioned the theft to Rob, one of our members, and explained that, unless the stereo could be recovered, he and his friends would have nothing on which to play the records and tapes that they brought into the club. "Leave it with me," said Rob, "I'll come back to you later." A couple of hours later, he returned with the stolen equipment under his arm! Rob had realised that the theft would deprive him of the opportunity to play his tapes and records. "I knew who took it", he explained, "so I went and stuck one on 'im. 'You nicked my music' I told him. 'Don't you take my music.'" Time and time again, we find that once the young people realise that it's their subscriptions that help to pay for the equipment, and that damage or theft will rob them of some benefit or enjoyment, they behave much more responsibly. They don't need to be charged large entrance fees for this to be the case, either.

We believe that Christian youth work should be trying to offer quality at less expense than secular clubs. In many pubs and clubs, pool tables cost thirty to forty pence to play. In a church youth setting, it should be less; ten pence perhaps. Football machines can cost fifteen pence to play; at St Paul's youth club, our football machines are *free* to play. Neither do we insist on a deposit before loaning out table-tennis bats and balls. In 1985, we were charging ten pence to come into our club, while the local secular club was charging fifty pence.

I was trained to realise that atmosphere and attitudes

are more important than facilities in themselves. The caring way in which the group or club is run should make the users stop and think "Why do you do these things, that don't happen in a secular club? Why do you let us in when we have no money when the other clubs turn us away? Why do you never ban anyone?" Once these questions come to the surface, the time is right for the Gospel to be presented.

I'm sometimes asked whether different home environments require different approaches to your work. I always answer that all kids have energy, no matter where they live, and it needs to be released. In many middle-class areas, it must be tempting to run a club where the young people are encouraged just to sit and read. This, I'm sure must result in them feeling very stifled by parents and church youth leaders who - like school teachers - tell them not to run so much because "it's not dignified", or, "It's not nice". It will give them a sense of repression as they grow older.

Specific problems which are caused or aggravated by home, educational, cultural and environmental factors will be discussed later, in the second half of the book. But real change only comes about by changing *people*, and this is true regardless of cultural and environmental factors. In our youth club we try never to lose sight of that fact.

A major decision which every club has to take is which days to open. We tried a lot of different formats at St Paul's and, initially, the best seemed to be to run the club two or three nights per week, with church activities on the other nights. One of the club nights was Sunday, and the session would end in time for the Youth Service afterwards. Because the non-Christians had been relating to their Christian mates in the club all evening, it was easy to get them along to the service. Gradually we've expanded until there are clubs running five nights of the week, with fellowship groups on Tuesdays, and only Saturdays left free, though we may soon be experimenting with Christian concerts on the first Saturday of each month.

Many of the other problems which face a youth worker are really those of the club members, but they are problems with which the worker has to become involved if he or she is to be of any real help. Often the only help that's needed is making oneself available to accompany a young person to their dole office, their doctor, or into any other situation where they feel ill-at-ease, or unable to cope. For example, a lad called Charlie came into our club recently. He was over the moon about the council flat of which he'd just become the tenant. There was only one little dark cloud on his horizon: "It's a pity about the heating, though." The heating? What's the matter with it? "Well, I can't get it to come on. I've told the caretaker, but he doesn't know what's wrong either." In a situation like that, I was able to show Charlie some real Christian love by contacting the local housing officer on his behalf. Not only did I help him to get his heating seen to, but, by asking around the club, I was able to get him some furniture too!

Getting young people into the building is a problem for many clubs. Let me pass on a tip which is virtually guaranteed to fill any youth club with lively, excited young people. Ready? *All you have to do is to hold a disco.* Simple, isn't it? The trouble is, that discos have nothing to do with youth work. It's impossible for a worker to relate to young people with loud music and flashing lights all around. Many secular clubs are under the impression that they do a good job by running discos. "Look at the dozens of kids that we're keeping off the street," they say. Yes, but look at the disturbance to the neighbours, caused by the noise level; and consider the noise and disturbance that's caused when the disco ends, and a hundred or more young people are let out – late at night – into a tranquil residential area. Not only is it not good youth work, it's not worth the complaints and bad feeling that it generates in the surrounding neighbourhood.

Young people are attracted legitimately by the

atmosphere of a club; by the people who attend the club; by the workers; and by the programme that's run. There's no short-cut to successful youth work, and success isn't measured in numerical terms anyway. Few young people usually mean a better member-to-worker ratio, and that means that the workers can *really* get to know the young people.

The opposite problem, which sometimes arises, is when the club is attracting *too many* young people. Often the problem can be solved by opening more nights, with the age range split between the two nights. But, unless the size of the club is really too small for the numbers, a better solution might be to take advantage of the large attendance, and to restore a better member-to-worker ratio by recruiting more workers. (Opening extra nights would probably require more workers anyway.)

There are often Christians who live in the suburbs who commute to the inner-city every day for their work. Those people need to be persuaded to stay on in the inner-city, perhaps for one night per week. It's a sacrifice for them, and it doesn't happen very often; but it's probably the only way forward in that situation.

Trying to manage without the necessary staff is just impossible. Many is the time when our club has been so full that there have been queues to use the pool and table-tennis tables. I've just had to turn to John Pearce and say, "All we can do is to make sure that we have a good epilogue tonight, and that they hear the word of God. We can't do any real person-to-person work, but I suppose we should be grateful that they're here at all."

It's a common problem, in many clubs, to have a shortage of helpers. Having people to collect sub-scriptions, and to run a canteen facility, on top of the actual job of supervising and working with the kids requires more staff than the average club can muster. At St Paul's, we're probably better off for workers than many clubs, but we don't believe in using workers to do jobs that aren't really youth work, and that can be done as well by the young people themselves.

When we needed someone to run our canteen – rather than have my staff burdened with the responsibility – I asked a group of four unemployed young people if they'd like to take on the job. "You can be bums all your lives, or you can try to make a go of something for yourselves," I told them. I didn't give them any money to get started, though one of our full-time workers gave them a lift to a cash-and-carry to purchase their basic stock. Now they're running our canteen as a business of their own. Not only is it saving us wasted staff time, but it's giving young people responsibility – power over their own lives. What could have been a problem has been turned into an advantage. It's one more example of positive Christian caring.

Our club canteen has a special place in my heart – and not just because I've got a sweet tooth for chocolate bars. When I became fully involved in the club again, in 1979, I noticed a young lady working in the canteen. Her name was Anne and, after I plucked up my courage, I asked her to 'go out' with me. To cut a long story short, two years later, she became my wife.

I felt that God had got my life back together again. In the areas of church, job and relationships, my life was beginning to be more fulfilled.

8

PROGRAMME AND EXPANSION

"What does this life offer you?" I asked. "Music? Sex? Drugs? Alcohol? Violence? That's all you hear about, or want to hear about, isn't it? If you helped an old lady across the road, no one would be interested. But if you were in a fight last night, you're a hero for a day; everyone wants to know about it.

"We live in a world today where hurting people, and embarrassing people, is more acceptable than helping, encouraging or caring for people. We fill our lives with rubbish – all the things that are harmful – not the things that are beneficial. We don't think of other people in terms of their growth and friendship; we look at them in terms of likes and dislikes, hatreds and jealousies."

The forty or fifty young people standing around, or sitting on tables, were listening intently. It was a Freedom Gate service, on the first Sunday in March, 1986. Behind me, the newly-completed mural with its dove, cross and world symbols made its non-verbal statement – God died for this world, and his Holy Spirit is active in it today.

"We were made by God to have love in our lives – love for our fellow humans, irrespective of class, colour or religion," I continued. "We were made to care for, and to help, one another. But look how far we've fallen. The Devil – and believe you me, there *is* such a supernatural being – has twisted this world, and twisted your lives.

"There's a hole in your lives, because God made you. It's an empty loneliness that cannot be filled by anything except God. It's like doing a jigsaw puzzle and finding, at the end, that there's a piece missing. It ruins the whole picture! Your life is ruined because you have a piece missing.

"Jesus is holding out his arms to you and saying to you, 'I'm the one! I'm the part that is missing in your life. Here, take me!' What are you going to say back to him? He's saying that he wants to make your life full. That's what he's saying to you tonight. Now, what are you going to do about it?"

And that, in its entirety, was my 'sermon'. We'd previously had a piece of drama, a couple of songs, a Bible reading, and a short prayer. Before and after, all the Christians in the club had met to commit the service to the Lord, and to pray that its message would strike home. It was a curious experience, praying in our tiny office, with the background noises from the rest of the club almost drowning out our words.

It's too easy to think of this sort of evangelistic event as the be-all and end-all of Christian youth work; but it's pointless converting young people unless you have the resources to disciple them properly, or they'll simply backslide again. And there are the other important aspects of youth work to be considered too: the importance of helping young people to get along with each other, and to relate better to adults.

We need to demonstrate Christ's love by helping young people to grow in confidence and in their ability to understand both themselves, and what is going on around them, before we can earn the right to expect them to seriously consider what we have to say about their spiritual life. It was only because I'd begun to earn that right – and took the trouble to communicate the Gospel in a simple way that they could follow – that they even bothered to listen.

Christ is concerned, not just for peoples' souls, but for the whole person. We need to share that concern, and to keep the various objectives of Christian youth work in balance. That's why a well-considered *programme* is important.

Trying to run a club without a programme is like

trying to build an aeroplane without a blueprint. When it comes to deciding what activities should be included in the programme, the best way to start is simply to ask the young people themselves. That's why we need our monthly members' meetings to determine short-term aims and objectives of the club, over and above the objectives that I've just outlined.

Obviously the kids have very little involvement with the spiritual input into the club, but we give them responsibility for practically everything else. There is an agenda that we pin up in advance, outlining the topics that we want to discuss, and the young people can add further ideas of their own. The current agenda, for example, includes 'drugs' – the use of which, we want to spell out to the members yet again, is one of the few things that we won't tolerate on the premises. Also discussed are any new activities which we are thinking of introducing into the club.

The members' meeting is still a fairly new idea, but already it seems to be working better than our old system of dealing with members' suggestions on an ad hoc basis. Unfortunately, at our first meeting – to which twenty members showed up – the most popular suggestion was to have a disco! I expressed my reservations about discos, adding – in particular – that a disco would attract a lot of non-members who might cause damage to the club, and spoil it for the regular members. The members said, "Yes, we realise the problems, but let's try it once and, if we *do* have any problems, we won't ask for a disco again." I thought that was a fair proposition and – rather than refuse and rob the members of power in their own lives – we agreed.

Other suggestions that have come out of members' meetings are the provision of weight-training and circuit-training. I was fortunate in having a worker in the club who could lead circuit-training, and I knew a friend who had experience of supervising weight-training. The following Monday, I had £150 worth of weights in the club. Within a matter of days, two two-hour periods of circuit-training had been introduced into the programme. Because we had space available in the coffee-bar, I was able to run weight-training in there, concurrently.

There can be problems when activities are over-subscribed. A few years ago, table-tennis became so popular that we ran out of space in which to put the tables. In the end, we were able to hire the hall of a near-by school specifically for table-tennis, and our own club could revert to being used for a more balanced programme. Strangely, the next craze was dominoes! It was very popular, especially with the West Indians. Fortunately, the game took up less space than table-tennis.

Other local clubs have, between them, an astonishing range of activities from drama to judo, via rock-climbing and ice-hockey. All these facilities can become available to members of our club, either through arranging to take a party of our members along to another club, or by arranging for a tutor to teach the activity in our own club. We don't *compete* with other clubs, we're simply in the business of meeting needs.

Though physical activity plays a very large part in our club's activities, we also include discussions. Each month, we have a theme which is carried through. If, for example, the theme was unemployment, we would put up posters and invite outside speakers to come and talk about the subject. Perhaps we'd begin towards the end of an evening of physical activity, when the members had exhausted much of their physical energy and were ready for a more subdued discussion. Beginning late would mean that the discussion could be open-ended, and anyone who wanted could stay and explore the subject into the night.

Outings and weekends away are always popular. One of the earliest outings that I organised was to take a group of lads to Hastings. Now, when I say that *I* organised it,

93

what I really mean is that I discussed the trip with the lads and, wherever possible, delegated the preparation. "Who's going to book the mini-bus? Who's going to order the food?" I asked. Sure enough, different lads came forward – tentatively at first – to volunteer for the different jobs. I had to give them a bit of help the first time but, when we went back the second year, they organised the whole trip themselves. Now, five years later, they still go down to Hastings every year. "Have you not thought of going somewhere else for a change?" I asked them one night. (I was worried that I had mechanically taught them how-to-go-on-trips-to-Hastings, rather than shown them the principles involved, which could be applied to trips elsewhere.) But Hastings has almost become their second home now. "We know where all the pubs and clubs are – and where to go to look for all the girls!" they say.

It's extraordinary what can be done once a youth worker has – first time around – given them a little help and built up their confidence, so that they can take responsibility in their own lives. To go on holiday with their mates, instead of their parents, is actually an enormous step for a young eastender to take. It's an example of real growth taking place through Christian open youth work.

Another more up-to-date part of our programme is the video-drama project. This started up when we got a £2,000 grant from a charitable trust to purchase a video-camera, recorder and monitor. This rudimentary system can produce quality television pictures – synchronised with sound – for instantaneous playback. It has endless possibilities, in that it only takes a few minutes to learn how to operate, but a whole lifetime to learn how to use well. Few young people fail to be absorbed and excited by their first encounter with video.

Video documentary has wonderful potential for highlighting social situations, aiding communication and helping to initiate change. But video offers great potential for drama, too. It can also be an objective

94

outside eye, enabling us to focus on how we are seen by others, and how we relate to others. It's difficult for any person to become aware of their basic mannerisms, way of speaking and walking, or even to be fully familiar with their own physical appearance. Their own view on the world directly around them is through a pair of eyes in the front of their faces. Mirrors and reflections in glass or water can give them a slightly different perspective – putting them in the picture, as it were – but video opens up their own immediate world to them in a revealing new way.

For example, young people, simply through being videoed for a few minutes walking, talking and taking part in a range of activities, can become aware of how they are perceived by others. They may discover, say, that they speak less clearly than they had believed, that their side profile indicates that they could usefully lose some weight, or that the way they slouch puts across an attitude that they would find repellent in others. Video is probably the best tool available for a youth worker who wants to increase young people's self-awareness.

After the initial enthusiasm has started to wane, and the members have become accustomed to viewing themselves on video, a whole range of further uses are possible. For example, if a group of young people were becoming constantly involved in arguments at home, they could 'role-play' the situation, taking it in turns to be themselves and each other's parents. That role-play, in itself, would make them more aware of their parents' position; but playing back a video of the arguing, with another young person role-playing the father figure, would enable them to learn something about their contribution to an argument and its background. Being able to go back and rerun parts of the mock argument is a particularly valuable facility. The same technique could be used, say, with a group of unemployed young people, who could improve their employment prospects by videotaping mock job interviews and playing back to analyse where they could have presented themselves more favourably.

'Girls on Film' was the title of a song – with a rather risqué video – by the group Duran Duran. But girls can be helped to overcome their stereotyped roles through the use of video equipment. Girls often experience seeing themselves on video in a very different way from boys. Their shyness often contrasts with the boys' exuberance, partly because they have been conditioned to feel anxious about their appearance. In planning a video-drama project, a mixed group might well be dominated by the boys; but, allowed to work separately as an all-girl group, more personal issues – like relationships, pregnancy, school and family life – will begin to emerge in contrast. A lot of preconceptions about the role of women in society are formed through the medium of television. Video provides a powerful medium through which these preconceptions can be confronted.

Some people dismiss the possibility of using video in their own youth work situation as an expensive pipe dream. But compared, say, with the wages for even a part-time worker, the cost is relatively small. It may prove possible to get a grant to buy the equipment; we got one from a charitable trust, but perhaps a local borough might be co-operative, once they see that there is a real need. Once acquired, perhaps a church could borrow their young peoples' video equipment, in order to video special services, anniversaries, etc. This could certainly be an 'ace card' in persuading a church to buy the equipment for the club, if the local authority declines to put up the money.

For St Paul's club, the 1980s have been years of growth and change. In 1981, St Paul's church combined with another local church – St Barnabas. The reasons for this had nothing to do with the youth project; it was simply a question of economics. The design of St Paul's church building made it very difficult to maintain, but – just 200 yards down the road – St Barnabas church was languishing with a small congregation, while its building was much more compact and easier to maintain. With a bit of legal formality, the two churches were officially combined.

In consequence, our youth project found itself with a second church hall. Although the old St Paul's church building was sold, the church hall was not; it still remained in the control of the new St Barnabas with St Paul's PCC, but we'd now acquired the St Barnabas hall as well. The PCC decided that it didn't really need two halls, so it officially handed the old St Paul's hall over to the youth project – lock, stock and leaky roof!

Now, when I'd rejoined St Paul's youth project in 1979, I'd said to God, "I don't want to go wrong again. Give me something for which to aim." I prayed and fasted, and God answered my plea. One of the answers that he gave me was that the old youth club would become a new Christian community centre. Shortly after the two churches merged, that promise started to become a reality. We received a grant to modernise and convert the old hall into a community centre!

Refurbishment commenced in 1984 and, while the old hall was closed, we shifted our youth club to the St Barnabas hall, running for two nights per week. The aim was that, when the modernisation was completed, we'd shut down operations at St Barnabas and move back to St Paul's hall. But God had other ideas!

While we were based at St Barnabas, he fulfilled two other promises that he'd made to me: local people became much more involved – as part-time and volunteer workers – in the running of the club; and a second full-time worker, Nick Simpson was appointed to work alongside me.

The St Barnabas club took off in such a big way (as a result of putting into practice the principles in this book) that the local youth officer asked me to give a hand with another, statutory club in the area – called Clapton Rangers. The youth workers there were all part-time and I was asked to take on the administrative work that really needed to be done during the day.

That was in 1985 and, in that year, we acquired our *third* full-time worker, Kevin Coleman. Though Kevin was intended to be our outreach worker (as a replacement for Pete Ellem, who's gone on to work at a local secular club) he has found it possible – especially during winter, when few young people can be contacted on the streets – to combine his outreach work with occasional club work at Clapton Rangers. As with Pete Ellem's move, it represented a wonderful opportunity to take a Christian presence into a secular club.

In February 1986, St Paul's club reopened, and I found myself running youth clubs on three different sites. Of course, restarting St Paul's again after a six month lay-off was not unlike beginning a totally new club. We had to sit down and take many of the same decisions that would have to be taken for a project starting up from scratch: which nights to open; open/closing times; age range of members; subscriptions and membership fees; finding extra workers; storage space; finance; club records; insurance; coffee-bar facilities; first aid; and the programme for the first night. Fortunately we didn't have to face the main problems of a new club – those of finding somewhere to meet, and establishing a working relationship with the owners. We *were* the owners!

A National Association of Youth Clubs (NAYC) publication entitled *No Kidding* suggests that, before opening a new club, one must first establish that there is a need by discovering: what provisions already exist; what do parents think about the idea; how many young people are there in the catchment area; and what kinds of activities do young people want. If we really *had* been new, we could have applied to the local youth officer to register with him, and we'd have received a £300 starting-up grant. (That's worth knowing, if you're thinking of setting up a new youth project at *your* church.) Once registered, a club can make application for future grants of up to £1,000; and it can apply for as many grants as it needs.

But we were simply restarting a club that had run successfully for nearly twenty years, up until six months previously. We were committed to reopening regardless of the need, since we had received – and spent – our grant for the modernisation. But the conversion had taken longer than expected. Would we have lost the interest of the local young people in the meantime? Would it prove to be a mistake to open with an almost-complete five-night programme from the beginning? Sure, we were experienced in this sort of work in this area, but had we bitten off more than we could chew? Were we being too ambitious?

We were opening in direct competition with *ourselves* and our activities at St Barnabas, and Clapton Rangers: would we now find that we'd reached saturation point and that we simply took young people away from the other two clubs? To our great relief, our fears were groundless. Fifty young people turned up on our opening night, largely by word of mouth; and hardly any of them had been going to the other clubs.

Now that we are open again, there are a number of factors to be considered if the club is to continue to run smoothly. We have to keep reviewing: the needs of our members; how to relate to other clubs, as well as the relationships within our own club; whether the club is integrating disabled people, ethnic minorities and females; the need for and cost of extra equipment; how to get the balance right between workers and members; transport, publicity and advertising needs; relations with the local press and the public and dealing with any complaints; and, finally, managing the management committee!

Any club has to keep asking itself, "What can we offer that will attract and appeal to young people at their own level?" and to keep updating the programme accordingly. Another major question is, "How much will the young people pay for it?" We decided on a fifteen-pence admission charge; or the young people can elect, instead, to pay a fifty-pence membership fee, and be admitted for ten pence thereafter. This is a lot less expensive than many other clubs, which gives us an advantage in terms of making it easier to attract young people who would not be able to afford high entrance fees.

Our staff seems to be increasing all the time. Though we officially have only three full-time workers, two of our part-time workers have no other employment, and work in the club without payment for the rest of the working week. We believe that it's important to get a mix of workers which reflects the types of young people who come into the club. We're short on black workers at the moment; we have only one part-time black worker, while approximately sixty per cent of our members are black. Only about ten per cent of the members are girls and we will shortly be recruiting a new full-time female worker, so that our staff team is representative of the women at the club.

As younger members get older, there may be a danger of the whole club catering for too old an age range. We as a club or as a church, will soon need to introduce the provision for people to *move on* to an older group, a twenties group, in order to have the space to let in new members at the younger end. We'd like to think that one of the reasons why we keep our members for so long is that we give them some control over their own lives. We don't impose on them in the club, and we keep our rules to a minimum. We do our best to keep the programme fresh, with new ideas constantly being tried out and put into regular use.

One innovation for us is a home-computer. It's just arrived so we've not really worked out the best way to use it yet. It would be nice if it could be connected to the local Job Centre, so that members could use it to check on any new vacancies, as they come in; but I suspect that there'll be some bureaucratic reason why we're not allowed to do that. We'll certainly use the machine for computer games, and a good deal more besides. It's good to use up-to-date technology, if only to present a contemporary and relevant image to the young eastenders.

The young lads who come to the club are anxious to increase the number of girls attending, so we'll have to give some thought to programme innovations – such as a self-defence class – which will make them feel more welcome. That's where our new female worker will be able to come into her own. A five-a-side football team, training during the regular evening club, and a parent-and-toddler club, probably running on a weekday afternoon, are in the pipeline. We've already got a playgroup running five mornings per week, though it's the only activity that takes place in the club that's not run by Christians.

One new addition to the programme that's still in the planning stages, is an afternoon meeting for unemployed people. They would not necessarily have to be young people; it would be good if they were older people, whom we could recruit as voluntary workers to help in the club. They could even be used to help the mentally disabled group, which we're thinking of running for three afternoons per week.

There's a lot going on at St Paul's club, but basically it's all grown within the last five years. If it can happen in Hackney, it can happen anywhere. All it needs is the vision; and that seldom comes except through prayer.

Remember though, that activities are not *in themselves* youth work, but simply a *vehicle* for that work. To be effective youth workers, we need to move away from considering just the activities, and to begin to consider the *issues* – because it is *issues* that touch and challenge the way we all live our lives and relate to each other.

There isn't the space to give more than a brief outline of some of the major issues facing youth workers today, but the seond half of this book will seek to help youth workers – and anyone who is sympathetic towards urban youth work – to begin to think out the issues for themselves. Where appropriate, I've suggested publications where further help can be found.

PART TWO

9

EDUCATION AND HOME ENVIRONMENT

Last week, I was talking to a nine-year-old white girl at St Paul's club, when an Indian boy walked in through the door. I was startled when the girl began to wave her hand in front of her nose, as though someone had just let off a stink bomb. With her eyes, she gestured to the boy and said, "I don't know what that blacky's doing in here. They stink!"

I couldn't believe my ears at first.

"But if you cut them," I said, "they bleed, just like you. Because they eat different food, the fact that the strong spices can sometimes be smelt on their breath is fair enough. It would happen with anyone, be they black, white or yellow."

It was with her next comment that the penny began to drop. It was the way she began, "My mummy says..." that was the give-away. It became clear that her racist attitudes had not been thought out by her, but simply copied from her parents.

I think that many people just take on board their parents' attitudes. In Hackney, many young people vote for the Labour Party, simply because their parents have always done so. If their parents say that blacks stink, they believe that blacks stink. Someone like that nine-year-old girl may be in our club for ninety minutes per week, and in her home for ninety *hours* per week. A fat chance I've got of ever influencing her more than her parents!

Adopting parental values, instead of taking the much more important step of discovering values for themselves, often prevents young people from developing their own personalities fully. They need to be brought up to be themselves, and to be aware of their own identity. Copying parents can be a very destructive process.

Graham Salt's dad has been in and out of prison all his life, and Graham is going exactly the same way. One of their favourite tricks is for Graham to get himself a job in a shop or factory, and then to figure out – from the inside – where all the alarm systems are located. Then his old man goes back one night and burgles the place! Graham was once employed at the local dog track, where he used to dope the best dogs so that his dad could win a lot of money by backing the outsiders! Graham doesn't fully realise that what he's doing is wrong, because thieving and fraud have always seemed like normal features of his environment and culture.

On Kingsmead estate, a group of eight-year-old children stole a milkman's moneybag and ran off to give it to their mother. Mum gave them fifty pence each out of the bag, and kept the rest for herself! If she doesn't care – if she doesn't try to give her children a right set of values – what chance do they have of growing up to be well-adjusted adults? When children are exposed to such environmental factors, so early in life, it's difficult for them to change later.

I could give dozens of examples of people known to me personally who have personality defects as a result of their traumatic upbringing. But the clearest example is one I was taught at college. Here's the family background of a notorious criminal. See if you can guess his name, and the crime that he committed:

His mother was a widow who had two other sons, including one from a previous marriage. Both these brothers were in care. His mother worked during the day, so he was cared for by neighbours and friends. When he was three-years-old, his mother couldn't cope anymore, so he too was placed in care.

The mother remarried, and she had him back. He became very fond of his step-father. At the age of eight, his mother and step-father separated. He was a latch-key child; so many times he came home to an empty house. They moved from the country to live with the eldest brother, who was married, in the city. At thirteen, he was aggressive and didn't fit into school; they all laughed at his country accent, so he played truant.

He was unloved by his mother, who gave him distorted values of what family life was like, and allowed him no opportunity to establish values of his own. He became beyond his mother's control, and was kept for psychiatric treatment in an institution.

At the institution, they said that he was tense, withdrawn and lived in a fantasy world. This could have been because of the lack of power in his real life. He was put on probation, and sent to a child-guidance clinic. He felt rejected by his mother, though – at the age of seventeen – she took him back to the country. She'd had a string of lovers and husbands; she told lies whenever it suited her; she cared little for her children, and she showed it.

At seventeen, he'd lived in twenty-three different dwellings, in five cities; he'd been to five institutions, and educated at twelve different schools. He joined the Forces, but this didn't help. He went out of his way to cause trouble, and was court-martialled. At the age of twenty he defected to the USSR, where he married, but couldn't stay. Near suicidal, he came home showing signs of mental illness. At the age of twenty-three, he shot President J.F. Kennedy. *His name was Lee Harvey Oswald.*

If a child lives with criticism,
He learns to condemn.
If a child lives with hostility,
He learns to fight.
If a child lives with ridicule,
He learns to be shy.
If a child lives with shame,
He learns to feel guilty.
But if a child lives with tolerance,
He learns to be patient.
If a child lives with encouragement,
He learns to be confident.
If a child lives with praise,
He learns to appreciate.
If a child lives with fairness,
He learns justice.
If a child lives with security,

He learns to have faith.
If a child lives with approval,
He learns to like himself.
If a child lives with acceptance,
and friendship,
He learns to find love in the world.

(Author unknown.)

Education is a problem for many parents. I think that educational standards have risen so much in the last couple of decades – even in an area like Hackney – that many parents are far less educated than their children. They place great store, instead, on what could be called 'life wisdom'. Most adult eastenders have been through a great range of experience, both good and bad, in their lives. It's natural, I suppose, that their children should reject conventional education in favour of experiencing life for themselves. If a parent has suffered poverty, divorce, bad housing, and a spell in prison, chances are that their children will take the same route, and end up in the same life-scarred state as their forebears. I don't know of any way of breaking the vicious circle, other than by introducing the transforming power of Jesus into their lives.

Children can't get much help from their parents in formal education because the parents have forgotten – through disuse – all the redundant knowledge that they learned at school. Even if they show willingness, the parents soon become unstuck with the metric system. "What's this?" they say. "I don't understand all these metres and kilometres. What is it in feet and inches?" When it comes down to even the most simple algebra, the parent is even more stumped.

But sometimes the church can help. I know of one lad at St Paul's club who was having problems at school, with his Maths. His parents – who are Christians – were unable to help him, but they knew someone else at the church who was good at Maths, so they were able to arrange a little extra tuition. That's just one example of how the collective knowledge of a whole church can become available to any individual member, just for the asking. It's a profound and effective demonstration of God's love being manifest in a practical way.

How different it is from when I was at school. I remember never being able – or willing – to do the homework. I'd cheat and copy it off someone else. I'd get caught quite regularly. "You're not clever enough to do this, Stow. Who did you copy it off?" the teacher would ask. It didn't do much good for my self-confidence!

It's surprising how little the young people in the club talk about school. I can sense that they're just not interested. It seems that, once they've finished for the day, they just want to forget about it. It seems like an imposition for them; some kind of punishment for having been born. The young people's attitude to education is perhaps summed up by the Pink Floyd song, 'Another Brick in the Wall':

We don't need no education,
We don't need no thought control.
No dark sarcasm in the classroom,
Teacher! Leave those kids alone!

Exams seem irrelevant to children with low career expectations. "I can't see the point of this," they say. "How's it gonna help me getta job on the building site, with me dad?" There are exceptions of course; some of them are very interested in computers and modern technology. But the old route of 'following in father's footsteps' is still very much the norm for many families. That makes it very difficult for a dad who's out of work to encourage his children to work. In that situation, he's got enough hang-ups of his own – about being a poor breadwinner – and is so despondent and filled with despair that he's unable to give hope for the future to his son or daughter.

The main influence in a child's life comes from the home, but too many parents still look to school as the be-all and end-all of their children's education. "If my son's bad, it's not my fault," they say, putting the blame on the teacher. It's the parents who need to be re-educated – regarding their attitudes to schooling – and the local church is one of the few bodies that can help to bring about that re-education.

The idea that learning doesn't have to be a painful experience often seems alien to teachers and pupils alike. Perhaps some teachers have so much trouble keeping order in their classes that they don't have time to try more effective teaching methods. If they did, pupils might find that learning can actually be an *enjoyable* experience. It never was for me until I got to college and could relax in lectures, with my feet on the table. Maybe teachers and pupils should call a truce, and look together for more interesting and enjoyable ways to carry out the educational process. At St Paul's club, we do our part by using multi-media to get the Gospel across in our Freedom Gate evangelism; and by using modern aids like computer and video to teach life skills.

Of course, a young person is influenced by other factors apart from parents and school. Take peer-group pressure, for example. Often a lad will come into the club either *doing*, *saying* or *wearing* something that all the other young people will turn around and copy. They want to be accepted, so they follow every passing trend. There is an extraordinary inferiority-complex prevalent in inner-city areas. People feel very insecure, and that's bad. There is a strong gang mentality, whereby the young people hang around in groups, and every member does what the group does; usually a course of action dictated by the stronger personalities in the group.

Gangs provide adolescents with a sense of identity and belonging, as well as a network through which opportunities and excitement can be shared. Gangs are not bad in themselves, though their actions can be. In the late sixties there was a good deal of intergang violence, with as many as two or three hundred young people involved, throwing bottles and bricks at one another – often over the heads of intervening policemen! The recent gang rioting in Tottenham and Brixton has received sufficient coverage in the national media not to require further discussion here.

Claerbaut, in his book *Urban Ministry*, says that in parts of the USA the gang problem is even worse than over here. There are accounts there of a high school where gang awareness and competition are so acute that different areas of the school are considered the 'turf' of certain gangs. One of the students found that a particular subject was taught in a classroom on the 'turf' of a rival gang. Rather than incur violence, he felt it wiser to accept academic failure. Of course, that sort of thing isn't happening in the clubs and schools of Britain . . . yet.

Younger siblings often learn from their big brothers. I know of one family where the eldest son goes away a lot. While he's away, the other sons – while they're not angels by any means – are at least bearable. But, as soon as their big brother returns, with his destructive ways, they totally change. They all want to be like him, so they all become destructive, too. Just when we thought we were really relating to the younger brothers, six months work is swept away in one week.

Pop stars are another influence, largely because music is so important in the lives of young people; though also because pop stars seem to have all the wealth, glamour and popularity which is missing in their own lives. Yes, we have members who walk around the streets with 'ghetto-blasters' – enormous portable hi-fis – balanced on their shoulders. Many of them feel very insecure without a permanent wall of portable sound. I think that many of them come to use the ghetto-blaster as if it were an instrument in itself. The music is *their* music, almost as though they'd written it and were playing it. So strong is the identification, that if someone says that 'their' music is good, they take pride almost in the same way they would if they were the recording artist. But they don't do so as an ego-trip, but more as a counter to their insecurities.

The music in itself is important to them because it expresses something which they themselves don't have the vocabulary to put across. Simon Frith, in the 26th June 1980 edition of *The Listener*, suggested that:

> Pop songs celebrate not the articulate, but the inarticulate, and the evaluation of pop singers depends not on words but on voices, on the voices around the words. In our daily lives, the most directly intense statements of our feelings involve not words but noises. We sigh and gasp, we moan, guffaw, cry, cheer and so on. We even measure the intensity, the profundity, the originality of our feelings by reference to our inability to find immediate words for them.

For a poorly educated eastender, that goes double! I think it's significant that most of the music that our members like features 'noises' rather than words, and compelling rhythms rather than tunes. Its poverty of melody ideally complements the poverty of East London. It is music to score drugs to; sexual in its pounding rhythm; and, harmonically, as bleak as an urban landscape. In short, it's the perfect soundtrack to inner-city life.

Young eastenders are influenced, not simply by the people around them, but by the deprivation of their home environment, and living conditions. Just look at some of the 1981 Census statistics: increasing industrialisation has led to a decreasing population in inner-London (at 2,500,000 people, the population is 500,000 lower than in the last census, in 1971). Of the 68,000 permanent 'residential units' in Hackney, more than 1,700 have no inside WC; and nearly 3,000 have no bath. (Though even this is better than neighbouring Newham, where more than 8,000 have no inside WC, and over 5,000 have no bath.) In Hackney, 75% of households have no car, and 33% of all households with dependant children contained at least one single-parent family. That's a phenomenal number of children being brought up by only one parent!

What the figures don't reveal is the untold suffering. Poverty takes many forms but, basically, they all come down to an absence of choice. No choice over where to live. No choice but the cheapest food. No choice but the cheapest clothes. No choice of job. No choice of furniture – make do with what you've got. No choice of when repairs get done – it's up to the council. The only choice is "Have what you've got or nothing at all."

Transport and communication in East London are poor compared with most areas of London. In the course of the preparation of this book, Mike Fearon came across to the club from his home in Finsbury Park. It's a journey of four miles, which he had no choice but to make by public transport. On one occasion, due to 'vandalism on the line', it took him ninety minutes to travel the first two miles. It was raining cats and dogs, or it would have been quicker on foot! There were no alternative means of public transport, and no way that he was going to get to the club before closing time, so he headed back. It took him another hour to get home. Leaving vandalism aside, the journey – which, at best, takes half an hour – can regularly take three times as long when, without warning, 'work is being done on the line'.

That's typical of many public transport routes in Hackney. The number 22 bus takes such a winding route that, during rush hour, it takes forty minutes to travel the three miles down to Liverpool Street station. Trains from Hackney Downs BR station run every ten minutes, but hardly a day goes by without a least three or four being cancelled without warning. The nearest London Underground station to the club is at least two miles away. Come up and see us sometime. But don't come by public transport!

Most of an average young person's education is informal. But in the deprived East End, a lot of that vital informal learning never takes place. For example, a lot of young people fail to better their lot because they've never learned basic communication skills. Such skills fall into five categories: listening, speaking, looking, reading and writing. Listening is an art that many people never learn, because they're too busy talking. It's common to hear young people 'opening their mouth with out putting their mind in gear'; they speak before they've worked out what they're going to say.

Young people are often uncertain about many things, not least on how to behave in certain circumstances – how to dress for an interview, how to speak to their boss, or what to wear for college. They need to be shown how to *listen* to other people's views, and to *observe* what other people do (or wear) in order to follow their example.

Young people often use body language without being fully aware of the meaning that it conveys. The way that they sit or stand tells a speaker the degree of interest they have in what is being said. A youth worker can help a young person to convey interest – often by simply deterring them from making negative actions, like turning their backs on a speaker!

An exercise to improve young people's awareness of body language, simply consists of observing two people in conversation for about five minutes, discussing a topic in which they have no interest. A group of young people could watch this 'live', or on video if the necessary equipment is available, and note down as many examples as possible of 'negative body language' (i.e. the speakers yawning, looking away, slumping in their chairs, etc.) A time of discussion could follow.

Decision-making at one level or another takes place practically everyday, by everyone. But, because it is such a common act, it receives little attention until people are faced with long-term decisions which may radically affect their lives. A youth worker can often help young people to learn how to take major decisions, such as whether to get married, whether to change job (if they have one!), whether to leave home, etc. Adults need to assess the existing degree of participation in decision-making, then to explore ways of increasing the opportunities for young people to *practise* decision-

114

making in more trivial matters, before the major decisions are reached. A club can do this by evolving a commitment towards encouraging new opportunities for young people to participate in the decisions concerned with running the club.

Sometimes, an adult allows the young person to make a decision – say, about how to spend a sum of money – *without defining any boundary or limit*. When a suggestion is made which the adult finds unacceptable, the young person is disappointed and begins to distrust the adult, who appears to have gone back on his/her word. Is it little wonder that adults often say, "We try to involve the youngsters, but it doesn't work," or, "When you ask them what they want, they never know anyway!"

Tension between young people and adults is not a new thing. It has long been felt that some young people have no real interests in life, and no real concern to find their roles in society. "Youth today loves luxury," said one critic. "They have bad manners, have contempt for authority, and talk nonsense when they should work. Young people do not stand up any longer when adults enter the room. They contradict their parents, talk too much in company, guzzle their food, lay their legs on the table and tyrannise their elders." That sounds like someone 'having a go' at me when I was a kid, but those words were actually said by the Greek philosopher Socrates, more than two thousand years ago! How little youth has changed since then, in the eyes of adults.

Traditionally, older people could teach the young by saying to them, "I have been young, but you have never been old," and the young people have echoed – from time immemorial – "Yes, but you've never been young in the same environment as us!" But that's more true today than it's ever been before. The blow to adult authority comes from the changes which have occurred in post-war society – particularly the advent of the distinctive 'rock culture'. Informal learning from adults has become a much more difficult matter.

"Youth is a rehearsal for maturity," according to the

National Youth Bureau publication *Rehearsing to be Adults*. "In the family, in the school, in the club, we find out what life is going to be about." The development from childhood to maturity takes place in a social environment. It is the interaction of *personal growth* with *social background* which creates many of the tensions in family relationships. The academics told me at college that the transition from child to adult involves several features:

- achieving an appropriate dependence/independence pattern;
- achieving a sense of belonging;
- acquiring an appropriate sex role;
- developing intellectual skills and concepts;
- attaining economic independence;
- developing a conscience, morality and a set of values.

Of course, most of the young people in our club – and many of the workers too, for that matter – would not have a clue what all that meant. But they are all things which the young people do, without seeing them in such academic terms. They are basically all to do with young people finding their *roles* in society.

A further aspect of 'growing-up' involves learning to use leisure time, at a time when leisure patterns in society are changing. Since the war, our leisure industries (cinema, theatre, concerts, etc.) have been youth-orientated; though that begs the question "What exactly *is* leisure?" Kenneth Roberts in his book *Youth and Leisure* observes that "one element of leisure is a type of time – spare or free time, the residue after physically necessary acts such as eating and sleeping, plus work and other social obligations... The second element of leisure is a type of activity – play or recreation."

Unfortunately, from my experience, in Hackney any attempt at definition breaks down. For the unemployed – who have neither the money to spare for play and recreation, nor any time which isn't free or spare – leisure is a meaningless concept. With time on their hands and nothing to do with it, apathy quickly sets in. For many who *are* employed, their employment is simply a means of filling up some of the long, empty hours. The wages they receive are so poor that there is no other source of recreation open to them other than an evening at St Paul's club.

In many respects then, we have a captive membership. For many, education and home life have been a disaster; our club is the only place left for them to run to, the only place where they can truly be themselves. Though we can help them through the traumas of entering adulthood, the best and loveliest thing that we can do for them – many of whom are still little more than children – is to introduce them to the one who said "Let the children come to me." In the end, that's what my open youth work in Hackney is really about.

10

HOMELESSNESS AND UNEMPLOYMENT

"It's terrible! I've had twenty-three different addresses in the last two years; bed and breakfast places; grotty 'hotels'; boarding houses; and bed-sits. Being homeless is awful. Most people, when they're kicked out, don't know what to do – how to find a place nor nothin'. It's bad. It's really hard."

Twenty-year-old Brian Jarvis lay back in his chair in my office. He's come through the worst of it, but it's painful for him to reminisce.

"When I first got kicked out, I stayed at friends' houses, a couple of weeks here, a couple of weeks there. When I found other accommodation, the DHSS helped by paying the rent; but there were a lot of hassles. Sometimes I wouldn't get nothin'. If you go up there and you don't know nothin' about 'Social', and what you're entitled to, they'll tell you you're not entitled to 'emergency money' when you *are* entitled. Sometimes they try to get rid of you, so they don't 'ave to pay out so much, know what I mean? You feel like you're poncing!

"You go up there (to the DHSS) and you see arguments and fights. You have to wait there – for maybe six hours – go up to the desk for perhaps six seconds, then go home empty-handed. It's soul-destroying.

"There were times when I wouldn't eat much – I'd spend my DHSS money on drugs," says Brian, in one breath destroying any pathos the rest of his tale might have held. But I felt that, perhaps, the drugs were only something he used to take his mind off his suffering.

118

"There have been times when I couldn't afford to buy myself any new clothes. It's hard. A lot of people don't realise how bad it is once you leave home, 'cos when you stay at home it's pure luxury; you get lots of things done for you, but people don't realise that. They still leave because they want to find out what it's like. But they regret it afterwards. There's nowhere like home."

Joyce Stewart is another sad case. Living at home, she spent all her dole money on clothes and drugs. Because she couldn't contribute towards her keep, her parents threw her out. Sure, she should have budgeted more wisely. But who was there to show her *how* to budget? No one had ever explained to her how she should plan ahead to have enough money to pay for food and accommodation. Spending the money was a means of breaking her out of her lethargy, and of restoring her self-esteem. But her parents didn't understand.

Joyce who's still in her teens, is now forced to sleep on sofas at friends' houses, moving on every few days. If she went to the DHSS, she'd be found accommodation; but they'd have no option but to pay for her to stay in one of the seedy doss-houses near Finsbury Park. Not only would she be separated from all her friends, but she'd be in moral danger. There's a red light area near there, where many of the girls in seedy accommodation have to ply the ancient trade to make ends meet. Then there would be the danger of attack by muggers. There are so many hard-up people around that it's impossible to get out of Finsbury Park tube station without being accosted and asked for "ten pence for a cup of tea". (But it's more likely to be spent on a 'meths sandwich'!) There's one chap who appears to sleep on one of the platforms, using a bench as his home.

If youth workers are to discourage young people from making avoidable mistakes and becoming homeless, we must learn to become more aware of the warning signs. We have to identify what the young person's most immediate real needs are; and that's something which forms part of the ongoing process of 'keeping an ear to the ground' and knowing what's really going on in the lives of the young people.

The reasons for leaving home in the inner-city are, I find, very diverse. Often it's simply a row at home. But it can be a long-term reason: i.e. the young person is constantly being beaten up – or even raped – by someone else in the home. It's not unknown for a girl to be homeless because she was working as a prostitute, tried to reform, and was thrown out by her pimp.

If someone is actually homeless, there is certain information that the worker needs to discover: did he/she leave home, or were they kicked out? Is this a new occurrence, or has this happened before? Does he/she have a particularly close friend/relative/probation officer/social worker? Why did he/she leave their last home? Would a youth worker's direct intervention in the home situation help the young person? The amount of help that a youth worker feels able to give in such situations should determine the sort of skills/information the worker needs to acquire in order to respond adequately.

If I'm approached by a young person who needs my help in such a situation, and I agree to help, then *I become part of the situation*. In that event, it's important that I'm fully in touch with my own feelings: am I supportive, helpless, manipulat*ive*, manipulat*ing* or simply totally removed from the situation? If the young person is looking to me for support, and I'm coming across as confused or unsympathetic, then I'm not going to be much help! The way that I put myself across can sometimes be more important than any practical help I'm able to offer. To give practical help in a reluctant way is often of less real benefit than to let a young person solve the problem by him/herself, while just being available to give information and advice.

The *GMYA/NAYC Training Pack* on homelessness suggests that it is important to know how the young person is feeling in the situation. These are some of the questions that may be going through a homeless young

120

person's mind: what about school/work? Will the police be involved? Can I refuse accommodation that I don't like? How long will it take to be rehoused? When can I legally leave home? (*At sixteen.*) Can I sleep in the youth club? (*Not a good idea.*) Shall I move in with my boy/girlfriend? (*Definitely not a good idea!*) If these or other questions are playing on a young person's mind, then the youth worker must get the young person to speak them out, otherwise they won't get answered, and the person may build up unrealistic ideas about what will happen to them. Tactful probing is a skill which a youth worker needs quickly to acquire.

A youth worker can often be of help in practical ways to a young person looking for accommodation, simply through keeping an ear open in the club for anyone who knows of a vacant room. A young person often needs help to understand what accommodation adverts in the newspaper really mean – like this one for example: '*S/C F/F flats avlb. H/C c/htg. £120–160 pcm exc. Refs reqd.*' Sometimes it's factual information they need, such as: "You can leave home at eighteen without your parents' permission, or at sixteen *with* their permission. Your parents can throw you out at sixteen, even though you can't legally rent out accommodation for yourself until you are eighteen!"

In the late seventies, the Greater Manchester Youth Association (GMYA) and the National Association of Youth Clubs (NAYC) jointly funded a three-year project on homeless young people, to explore the *process* of leaving home. The project found it impossible to discover any clues by which young people on the verge of leaving home can be identified: one has to wait until the tensions come to the surface and, all too often, that doesn't happen until the young person has passed the point of no return.

Research suggests that young people leaving home prefer the support of friends, and knowledge of their locality to the anonymity and loneliness of a strange town or city. The flood of young people descending on London looking for the 'streets of gold' has diminished to a trickle but - for native eastenders - they are still stuck with the deprivation that they have always known.

The report looked closely at the nature of the problem of young homelessness. Amongst its findings is the conclusion that:

> If the youngster fails to find appropriate help he is likely to turn to, or be picked up by, members of deviant or outcast subcultures. In other words, he/she is likely to be picked up and introduced to prostitution, to become involved in drug-taking, or to be initiated into various forms of petty criminality. Alternatively, he/she may simply drift into the world of the older single homeless, or become by association and finally by habit, yet another 'dosser'.

For the long-term homeless, realities become progressively distorted. They tend to 'package' themselves as deserving cases, often through exaggerating or lying about their background and, perhaps, eventually coming to believe their own lies to be truth. The picture becomes further distorted when homeless people are exploited by the media, for their dramatic potential. In the end, it becomes increasingly difficult for agencies working with the homeless to recognise the truly deserving cases. It's a trap that even Christian agencies can too easily fall into, even though the idea of 'deserving and undeserving cases' smuggles in the concept of moral judgement that Christians have no right to make. All homeless young people are deserving of our help, simply because they bear the image of our creator.

Here's some advice that a Christian involved in youth work could usefully give to a young person thinking of leaving home: Don't leave home in a temper, or after a row, because you might regret it later. If you do leave, make sure that you have plenty of money with you, (realistically, you will need well over a hundred pounds). If you decide to go to another town or city, possibly in search of work, try to go with a friend. Watch out for the government legislation which means that, under the age of twenty-six, you can only spend a maximum of eight weeks (less in many cases) in bed and breakfast accommodation in the same town.

A qualified youth worker can refer young people to hostels and other forms of accommodation (i.e. halfway-houses, reception centres, night shelters, etc.) if he/she believes that this would meet a young person's most important immediate needs. I'm fortunate that the nearest hostel for single homeless people is literally right next door to the club! The old St Paul's Vicarage has now been converted to sleep up to seven young people in single rooms. It was founded by a group of Christians from near-by churches, and operates under the name of Homerton Space Project. It aims to give young people the space they need to learn how to live their own lives.

"One of the first problems that we encountered", says Dave Greenwood, the project's chairman, "was that of actually defining homelessness. Does it mean literally not having a roof above your head? Or having 'no fixed abode'? Or sleeping on someone's couch? Or even living at home, but in moral or physical danger? In the end, we defined it as having no home, *or* having no secure or permanent dwelling, *or* having no safe place to stay. However, we only admit a person to the hostel after all possible reconciliation with the parents has been tried, and if he/she lives there with a view to being independent afterwards, and does not merely return home.

"There are many homeless people in the inner-city who are middle-aged workers with obsolete skills, or are people whose lives have been regimented (looking after an authoritarian parent or, not uncommonly, as a member of the armed forces). This type of person has acquired a lifetime of social habits which are not easy to break. It would be unfair then, to accommodate this type of person in a hostel alongside young people. Probably because of St Paul's strong traditions of youth work, we decided to open a hostel specifically for the second category of person, the homeless *young* person, between

123

the ages of seventeen and twenty-four.

"The management committee feel it important to achieve a balance in the house, and that the ratio of black/white residents should be a fair representation of the ratio of homeless people in the area. Statistically, men are three times more likely than women to be homeless; but, within the age range we cater for, the sexes are almost evenly balanced."

Obviously, there are pressures in any hostel, due to the shared use of kitchen and bathroom. Even with friends this is never easy: with total strangers, it's much worse.

A group of people who tried a youth work approach to housing homeless young people (with a hostel in South Manchester) found it difficult to arrange rotas for cleaning, since competence varies considerably, as do opinions about how soon after cooking, the pots and pans should be cleaned. Some people have perhaps never had to cook for themselves before, and their experiments can be devastating.

The *idea* of communal living is attractive to many young people, but they can't stand the reality! There are good mixes and bad mixes of people for any hostel, and it's often difficult to tell how a new resident will fit in. Only time can resolve that question. The more self-contained the accommodation, the fewer the problems caused by friction between the residents. Outside support for the staff, from a sympathetic management committee, is an important consideration when working with youth in a residential context, just as it is with other types of youth work.

The major dissatisfaction with a lot of hostel-dwellers is over the rules. In many secular hostels, the residents are treated like children. They have to leave during the day, return at a particular time if they want their evening meal, and be in bed by 10.00 p.m. This, naturally, causes a lot of resentment. Some of the comments of hostel-dwellers interviewed for the HMSO publication *Single and Homeless* are very revealing: "When you're in a cubicle, it's like being in a paper house – geezers doing

124

their toilet in your room"; "I need privacy"; "Clothes go missing as well here. You can't even put your knickers down without them going missing"; "They steam your letters open"; "When the weekend comes, you have got nowhere to go"; and "I'd love to know why there are all these rules".

Most hostels for young people do not offer the residents their own room, or allow them to cook for themselves. When the management committee of Homerton Space Project were planning their short-stay hostel, one of the primary decisions was that each resident would have their own room, which they could lock. It was originally intended that the young residents would eat communally for five nights of the week, but, when they complained that they'd rather cook for themselves, it was decided to reduce the level of communal eating to only one night per week. Many young people feel that there is a stigma to living in institutional accommodation. Homerton Space Project has tried to remove some of that by not giving their hostel a name, but simply an address – 51 Chelmer Road, Homerton, E9.

Because the committee members are all Christians, they want to provide a much higher standard of accommodation than a secular hostel, but without charging a higher price. This, of course, means a lot of fund-raising is needed to subsidise the rent; but this is accepted as part of the caring concern, as Christians, for young people in the inner-city. The project has not been without its problems. But it is exciting to see the church involved in the community in this way.

There is a strong correlation between homelessness and unemployment. The *Single and Homeless* report shows that 21% of all homeless people are homeless for employment related reasons, and 44% of those who are homeless and under twenty-five years old have no job. Homelessness is not only a major problem for young people, it's also a major problem for inner-city people. Young eastenders again have a double burden to bear.

Since the report was published, unemployment has

climbed dramatically, and it seems likely that many more people in sub-standard accommodation are in that situation simply because they cannot find a job. Without a steady wage coming in, they are caught in the poverty trap and cannot afford to improve their standard of accommodation.

It is the unskilled and semi-skilled who are worst hit by unemployment and, significantly, mainly the unskilled and semi-skilled who are homeless. The *Single and Homeless* report shows that 59% of the homeless had left school 'as soon as possible', and 43% have no training or skills whatsoever. But young people are particularly deprived, even amongst the total homeless population: 66% of those homeless and under twenty years of age have no training or skills. Even those *with* skills often find themselves drawn into unskilled work, because the lack of secure accommodation creates difficulties in maintaining regular skilled employment. Put another way, *becoming homeless renders people immediately vulnerable to unemployment.*

For a young person, a trip to the Job Centre is a depressing experience. Virtually every job card demands experience or skills that the young do not possess. Many of the wages offered are scarcely above supplementary benefit levels. The older people that they jostle with have lined faces that tell their tales of redundancies and dismissals. The idle chatter is of DHSS giros not arriving, of jobs held for a matter of days, and – above all – of the injustice of the situation: "It isn't fair that we have to suffer like this. We don't ask much of life, just a little money to buy food and decent clothes"; "They used us here for twenty years. Now they've got no use for us. They want us out"; "Oh, it's a free country all right. You're free to starve to death, 'cos there's no sod will help you when you're down"; and "They (the DHSS) give the impression the money's coming out of their own pockets".

Those four quotes are taken from Hackney people interviewed by Paul Harrison, for his book *Inside the Inner-city.* In his preface, Harrison says:

The inner-city is now, and is likely to remain, Britain's most dramatic and intractable social problem. For here are contained the worst housing, the highest unemployment, the greatest density of poor people, the highest crime rate and, more recently, the most serious threat posed to established law and order since the Second World War.

That's no overstatement.

Down at the local DHSS office, in Sylvester Road, there is usually a queue of despondent people who look like death warmed up. The rows of red Formica benches in the reception area are bolted to the floor, probably not so much to deter theft (who'd want one of the hideous things anyway!) as to thwart frustrated claimants from picking them up and hurling them at the thick perspex screens behind which sit the officials. Going up to the screen to talk to an official is like being in prison and going up to see a waiting visitor. No direct contact is possible; poverty might be contagious.

Benefits exist, but those entitled to receive them are left to their own devices to find out about them. It's like a game the DHSS play, except they always interpret the rules to suit themselves. It seems to be the same with local authorities too. I heard of an extraordinary Catch-22 situation where an Anglo-Indian gentleman wasn't allowed to become a teacher because the LEA wouldn't recognise his Indian degrees; but they wouldn't give him a grant to study at a British college because 'he was already a graduate'!

Though an unemployed young person is eligible for rent rebates and supplementary/unemployment benefit, the DHSS, the Department of Employment and local-government housing departments are often so under-staffed, and under so much pressure, that benefits can take a long time to be assessed. I know of two people who recently moved out of Hackney into the next borough. One of them was unemployed, but had to wait two months for his housing benefit to arrive, even though he had a friend to help speed up the process who worked for the DHSS! The second was employed, though on a very low income. Because he wasn't a priority case, he had to wait six months for his claim to be processed.

"Being homeless was awful, but being unemployed was worse," says Brian Jarvis. "You've got no money so you've got to go out and steal, to get money for food and clothing. I used to go down the Job Centre, and there'd be jobs offering twenty-five pounds per week, when I need a hundred pounds per week to settle my rent and pay my bills. I'm better off on the dole, know what I mean?" It's not unusual for young people to be driven to crime to make ends meet; though I suspect that 'moonlighting' – working, while still claiming benefit – is a more common occurrence. Unemployment is probably making criminals out of people who would otherwise be law-abiding citizens.

What can a Christian youth worker do about the problem? We can seldom find a job for a young person, but we can help to educate a young person on how to find a job for him/herself, and how to keep it. All that it takes is basic advice, such as: "Call people 'Mr', 'Mrs' or 'Miss', until they tell you otherwise; remember the name of the person to whom you are to report when starting a new job, or going for an interview; arrive on time, which will probably mean checking bus times, etc., in advance; smile, and look as though you're going to enjoy the experience of working for your living; and don't become too upset if workmates play jokes on you, such as saying 'go buy a tin of striped paint,' or 'fetch me a left-handed screwdriver'!" Often, older people don't tell young people the things that they need to know, because they sound too obvious. But it's better that someone is inadvertently told something repeatedly, than not being told at all; especially if it's something important.

The expectation when going to work is very high; but young people often become disillusioned when they find out that, in reality, most of the work for which they're ever likely to be considered is boring. But, at least, the person who has a job feels that they've finally made the transition from childhood to adulthood. I remember, for me, the great thing about going to work was that I was suddenly treated the same way as my father and working brothers. Now though, many young people are not given the opportunity to affirm their adult status with an honest day's work, so they continue to have little sense of self-esteem. They feel neither children nor adults; there seems, to them, to be nowhere that they fit in.

Young people who are working don't always understand what it's like to be unemployed. They feel that unemployed people don't really want to work; that they don't really look for jobs. Some employed young people that I know have made the mistake of thinking that it's so easy to find a job that they throw in the job they've got, expecting to get a new one next week.

It *was* like that when I started work in the late sixties; I had half a dozen jobs in three or four years, starting as a messenger boy in the post office, before becoming in turn: a tailoring worker, a cinema projectionist, a factory worker, and a shop assistant, before moving back into tailoring. But the days when an employee could turn around and say "I'm taking my labour elsewhere. I shan't have to look long either; there's plenty of firms crying out for staff" are now long gone.

A lot of the young people at St Paul's club have unrealistic expectations about the kind of work available to them. "Oh, I'm going to be a shop manager on one hundred and eight quid per week," I've heard them say, when they'd be lucky to get a job stacking boxes round the back of the shop, for a third of the money.

Of course, central government has attempted to cater for young people in need of jobs, but only through unrealistic measures designed to give 'work experience', but not real jobs. In September 1983, after a few pilot schemes, the Manpower Services Commission introduced a scheme of training and work experience called the Youth Training Scheme. A year-long YTS programme consists of: off-the-job training at a college of further education; planned work experience; an introductory programme; and on-the-job training. The bulk of the course is completed at the premises of a local business or manufacturing company, where – in theory – guidance and support is given to help the young person to become more self-reliant and self-confident.

In Hackney, a lot of young people resent the scheme. They believe that it exploits them as a source of cheap labour. The rate of pay – currently twenty-five pounds per week – is seldom more than the young person would receive on the dole. Many participating companies are able to skimp on the training element of the courses and to concentrate on using the young people to increase their production. The certificate that the young people receive at the end of the scheme is of dubious worth, and many young people find themselves back on the dole at the end of the year. It's left to youth workers like myself to help them to cope with the disappointments and feelings of having been abused – and to try to help them to regain their shattered self-esteem.

Many of the young people who initially refused to go on YTS because they wouldn't be paid enough money, are now going because of sheer boredom. Many of them have got into the habit of staying in bed till midday, and not going to bed till the middle of the night; I suppose that coming into the club breaks up the day for them. If nothing else, the schemes will retrain them in the discipline of getting out of bed and getting to a certain place by a certain time. But the feeling of being used as cheap labour causes a lot of resentment. I know of builders who've fired their labourers, who were earning a hundred and twenty pounds per week, in order to take on YTS trainees on forty pounds per week.

When the YTS trainees come into the club, they have more in common with the unemployed than the employed. With the latter, the topic of conversation often turns to buying new clothes, going away on holiday, getting a new car, etc. On these issues, the YTS trainees, like their dole-queue counterparts, have nothing to say; they don't have the money even to think about these things.

Unemployment and homelessness together remain major causes of tension and resentment amongst the young eastenders. The inner-city is hard and inhospitable to the poor and needy, just as Bethlehem was two thousand years ago, when an unemployed joiner and his pregnant wife found themselves homeless – but something good came out of that. I'm less optimistic about the prospects for today's young urban-dwellers.

11

VIOLENCE AND CRIME

Geoff Walker was built like a heavyweight boxer. About two years older than me – and twice as wide it seemed – he was a person whom everyone respected. No one had ever seen him fight, because no one had ever dared to try their hand with him. His legs were like treetrunks and it seemed that nothing short of a bulldozer could ever knock him down.

I hated him.

I must have been twelve at the time; it was a few months after I'd arrived at Upton House school. Perhaps I resented him because he never had to prove himself. The other lads respected him in a way that I envied. I wanted to *be* somebody, and one way to achieve that would be to knock down this big lump of dough.

"I'm not scared of him," I told my mates, but inside I could feel my stomach churning with apprehension.

In a fair fight, this Goliath would make mincemeat of me, so I knew that I had to win by dishonest means. For weeks, I waited for my chance. Eventually, one break time, I stalked Geoff across the yard until he was standing next to some chairs and tables which were being moved by the caretakers. The caretakers had gone for a tea break, and left them there. A quick glance around told me that there were no teachers about, so I grabbed my opportunity.

I sneaked up behind Geoff, and used a chair as a stepping stone onto a table immediately behind my unsuspecting opponent. The palms of my hands were cold and clammy as I clenched my fists together. Then, without warning, I swung at Geoff with both fists! Well, from the top of the table, I was a good few inches taller than him. I caught him across the face with a blow that I was sure would lay him out.

I nearly died when I saw that he was still standing, and was turning to face me. Oh no! I've really got it coming to me now, I thought. I had visions of him picking me up with one hand and using me as a rugby ball. And I didn't fancy the idea of being kicked around the playing fields.

In desperation, I began windmilling with both fists, hoping that he'd fall down. Though I don't think that I hurt him at all physically, I certainly seemed to strike a blow to his ego. Fear had always made the other lads be friendly towards him; but now, for the first time, someone was behaving aggressively towards him. It was more than his self-confidence could take.

"What are you doing that for?" he said in gormless disbelief, looking like a big sad teddy-bear. Then my punches began to take effect. But, instead of fighting back, he began to cry. He isn't that tough then, is he? I thought.

A huge cheer went up from around the yard. Few had seen the beginning of the fracas. Most didn't know that I'd climbed on a table top for advantage, and thought that I was beating Geoff in a fair fight. I was a hero for a day; and, for years afterwards, the other lads treated me with respect.

At home though, things were different. Like many of the young people who come into St Paul's club now, I lacked self-esteem. I felt so frustrated that, like many of our members, I wanted to go and smash something up, or attack someone; anything to release my pent-up aggression.

When I finally blew my top, it was over the business of my younger sister and I having the same bedtime. It happened one Saturday when I was about thirteen. My parents were going out that night. They would make sure that I was in bed before they went, but I wanted to come into the front room and join my brothers while my parents were out.

"Yeah, sure," said my brother Dennis when I approached him in the kitchen, "as long as you can get past Doreen's bedroom." My sister's room lay halfway between my bedroom and the front room. If Doreen heard me as I tiptoed past her door, then the game would be up. Either she would want to come through and watch TV too, or she would threaten to tell my parents that my brothers had let me join them. Either way, my brothers would insist that I remained in bed.

"No!" I cried out from my sense of repression. "*You* sort it out! I want to come through!" I was tired of being treated like a pet dog. I wanted the kind of respect that I'd won at school, through my fighting.

"Don't you get heavy with me," my older brother threatened. "Don't you try..." the voice trailed off as he saw me reach across the table and pick up a kitchen knife.

"You really *are* mad, aren't you?" he said, his eyes fixed on the blade. With a feeling of power, I leered at him, daring him with my eyes to make a move. He stood transfixed to the spot, uncertain of what he should do, but I soon made him shift! I lunged at him with the blade, and Dennis dodged back. The knife stopped in the air, where his stomach had been a half-second earlier. I could have stabbed him at that moment, without scruple.

My brother muttered an oath as I jeered at him. Then he turned tail and ran out of the room. He pulled the kitchen door shut behind him. I laughed. In my mind, I notched up another victory; another person to whom I'd proved my toughness.

Since I've been a youth worker, I've learned that those sorts of incidents are all too common. A lot of crime and violence takes place within the home. As one criminologist has put it: "You are safer on the streets than at home; safer with a stranger than with a friend or relative." Many violent acts are committed by persons who have been made to feel humiliated, ineffective and of no consequence.

Resentment often goes back a long way, and emotional upset at an early age can often result in inappropriately violent responses in later life. It's not just tension between brothers either; in fact, it's probably more frequent between parents. Self-esteem is often linked with sexuality, and a person made to feel sexually inadequate by their partner can sometimes respond violently.

For myself, my early teens were so rough that my acts of violence all seem to have merged together in my memory, like one long trailer for a Clint Eastwood film. Fighting would always make my day.

Some of the incidents were comic; I once beat up a lad called Steve Clarke and his brother Roland complained – so I beat Roland up as well! Other incidents were like stories from a comic book; I once went to a club on the Springfield estate and, single-handed picked a fight with the whole of a rival gang. They were all going to set upon me, but my own gang had infiltrated the club without them realising, and jumped them when they moved.

I'm not proud of any of it now, but at least it's given me an understanding of what it's like to live that sort of life. It's an experience that makes it easier to relate to many of the violent youngsters who come into our club.

I sometimes wonder if the young people are not sometimes more 'sinned against' than 'sinning'. Though they inflict misery in the lives of others, the 'others' are often their own peers, who 'do unto others' as much as they are 'done by'. The real evil lies less in their actions than in the social conditions which have made them the way they are. It is *that* that we should be condemning, as we love the sinner but hate the sin. Poverty and injustice are the real villains of the piece.

We need to develop legitimate opportunities for young men to flex their muscles and demonstrate their masculinity in ways other than socially-unacceptable aggression and violence. All the energetic and competitive activities we present in the club are designed to achieve this to some extent, but there is a limit to what we can do alone. And, even when the aggressions have been sweated-out of the young people, something is needed to fill the emptiness that's left. Ultimately, only Christ can fill the gap, but a lot of reworking of attitudes and lifestyles needs to begin, in most cases, to bring the people into a position where they can see Christianity as relevant to their needs.

Borstals and remand homes assist in redirecting the aggressive energy, with their emphasis on strenuous physical activity, but they seem to me to be too concerned with punishing and not enough with rehabilitating. There are exceptions of course. At one borstal in Falkirk, the inmates help to teach spastic children to swim – which helps to repay their debt to society in a practical way that encourages tenderness to take the place of hate. Penal institutions need to follow the lead of youth clubs, perhaps by getting older lads to organise recreational activities for younger boys in their spare time. Young people still in education could perhaps be steered away from violence by being given responsibility, and being encouraged to devote some of their time to communal needs – perhaps in place of some formal education.

Environment can play a large part in controlling violence, and physical design and decoration of buildings can play a significant role in reducing it. Dark, dank underpasses beneath main roads where unpleasant incidents can occur need to be replaced with small overhead bridges – as happens in Japan. Campaigning to bring that about is something that a more politically-orientated youth leader could do in this country.

On a smaller scale, the decoration of a youth club is a matter which every club can pay attention to, to assure that it feels light and airy, rather than dull or oppressive. Colour incidentally, is not just a matter of personal preference. Red is an aggressive colour, likely to *encourage* violence, while blue is a cold colour likely to lead to apathy. Green is a relaxing colour, well-suited to helping to iron-out the kind of tensions which lead to violence.

Colour plays an important part in making people feel welcome when they walk into a club for the first time. You never get a second chance to make a first impression, so you've got to get the colours right first time. Murals can also help to produce a soothing environment, particularly murals that, say, depict the history of minority groups that you may want to attract into the club. Murals or pictures of local landmarks give a club a sense of community; but don't get in a professional artist to paint them when the young people may enjoy doing them themselves. Care needs to be taken not to emulate the mistakes of British colonialism on a local scale; India is full of churches with memorabilia of British victories, and Indians who were killed in them! Not very tactful ...

Anything which may prevent violence from escalating is worth trying. For myself, once fighting had become my favourite pastime, I just wanted to find ways of hurting people more. I must have been twisted inside.

I remember one Sunday back in 1968, my skinhead gang met for a drink in The Stag, our local pub. One of our members explained, over our pints of lager, that his mother had been attacked the night before at a certain pub in Queensbridge Road, down in Bethnal Green. She'd been roughed up by some lads from the football team that frequented the pub. Her face was grazed, and she'd been bruised when they threw her out. Well, our gang wasn't going to stand for that; we decided that we would go down there and sort out the offenders – with our fists and boots.

To be quite honest, I wasn't very keen on this approach on this particular day – not because I didn't love fighting – but, rather, because it was my eighteenth birthday and I wanted to get drunk!

I remember the tension as we sat there in the

Queensbridge Road pub, waiting for the culprits to walk in. We'd changed into our 'bovver boots' in order to inflict the most pain during the fight. We had glasses of drink in front of us, to give us some Dutch-courage. You could have cut the atmosphere with a knife.

I was scared. There were only eight of us, and the football team was certain to outnumber us. Our only hope of victory was the advantage of surprise. We *had* to be ready to attack, going in hard at the first appearance of our foes.

"That's one of them!" went up the cry and, expecting the rest of his mates to be behind him, we went for the youth as he walked through the door. In an instant, we had all smashed our beer glasses and lunged at him with the jagged edges. Blood spurted everywhere as he was slashed, kicked and beaten to the ground. Trampling over him, we rushed outside to set upon the rest of his mates, whom we were sure were right behind him. But there was no one there.

The one guy had borne the brunt of the pent-up aggression of all eight of us. To be honest, I'd been near the back and – though I might have put the boot in a few times – I hadn't done him any of the damage with broken glass, which had left him lying still, in a pool of his own blood.

"You've killed him! You've killed him!" shouted an old woman as she saw the body. In a shot, we ran off back to our waiting van. One of our gang was shouting "My thumb! My thumb!" and his left thumb was hanging off – almost severed by the broken glass that had shattered when he'd rammed it hard into our victim. I wanted to be sick. We took our injured mate to Hackney hospital, but that was our downfall, because the police put two and two together and guessed that he was one of the attackers. He eventually 'grassed' on us all.

That incident was 'Skinhead Pete's Last Fight'. It was so horrific that it put me off violence for life. A few days later, I was walking down Homerton High Street when I felt a hand on my shoulder. It was John Pearce. You know the rest of the story – I told it back in chapter four. It was that fight in the Queensbridge Road pub that, indirectly, led to my becoming a Christian.

Several of the culprits – the lads who'd been at the forefront of the violence – were sent down for three months apiece. In the 1980s these sorts of fights are not uncommon, and some young people consider it prestigious to have served time for GBH (grievous bodily harm) or armed robbery. Violence escalates, as it did for me, from fighting with fists, to fighting with knives, to using any vicious object which comes to hand.

There have always been occasional fist fights at St Paul's club but, a year or two back, it started getting out of hand. I have a vivid recollection of separating two of our members, who'd had a disagreement, produced vicious meat cleavers – the sort used by butchers – and were about to go for one another with them. With a bit of help, I managed to disarm them, and we let the fight go ahead just using fists. It was the only way we could have got them to release their tensions and, once there was a clear winner, I could break it up without danger that they would simply go elsewhere and stage the fight as armed combat.

Carl, one of our part-time workers, was walking along Mare Street (the main road through Hackney) one day, when he heard someone behind shouting, "Stop him! Stop him!" Turning, Carl saw a young man running towards him, clutching a lady's handbag. Well, we get some strange people in Hackney, but Carl decided that this was a straightforward case of handbag-snatching, and brought down the thief with a very dramatic Rugby-tackle, and returned the bag to its rightful owner. Fearing that the thief might have an accomplice, he decided to let the thief go, before he was set upon himself.

I tried to discover if any of our members had been mugged. No one would admit it – or admit to being a mugger for that matter. I suspect that any would-be mugger would come off worst if he tried to tangle with any of the tough-looking lads that come into our club; but it wouldn't surprise me to discover that several of our members had done a few muggings in their time.

One of our girl members was followed down the street by a lad whom she was convinced was about to grab her handbag. With great presence of mind, she turned around and greeted her potential assailant: "Oh, it's you! Long time no see. How's yer brother?" She'd never seen the guy before, but he was so startled by the reaction that he walked off and left her alone!

To give some idea of the range of crime which takes place in Hackney, I'd intended listing all the crime reported in the local newspaper in a single week; but there was more crime reported in one edition than I've got room for here! A burglar escaping with £2,500 worth of jewels, or vandals causing £2,000 worth of damage at a local school, would cause a headache for the editors of most provincial newspapers, wondering which news story should have the biggest headlines on the front page. But those sort of stories are so common in Hackney, that they are tucked away near the bottom of the back page. The front page headline says 'Back On The Street', and explains that a new flood of prostitutes could swamp Stoke Newington's red-light district because of cutbacks in policing.

About the last thing that Hackney needs is a cutback in policing: Phil, another of our part-time workers, recently went to watch Arsenal play Spurs in a league match; at the end of the match, he witnessed a small group of young adults senselessly kicking the seats. There's a child-molester loose on near-by Kingsmead estate; though the parents know who he is, there's insufficient evidence for the police to make a move. At our Junior Youth Club, all the kids want to do is to fight all the time. Recently, a delivery van was parked at the end of my street and, while the driver was inside a shop arranging to unload, a gang of kids broke into the back of the van and were running down the street carrying stolen Weetabix boxes!

Hackney is only nineteen square kilometres in extent, but it must be nineteen of the roughest, toughest square kilometres on earth. In 1981, there were more than twenty-three thousand serious crimes in the borough; that's one for every three households. One person in every hundred was mugged. One household in sixteen was burgled. One car in four was stolen, or stolen from. That gives some idea of the world of crime in which young eastenders are born and raised.

Burglaries and muggings are primarily crimes committed by males, for the purpose of acquiring money and goods that can be sold for money. Often the money is needed, not for luxuries, but simply to buy food and to pay the rent. Paul Harrison points out that, in one twelve-month period, 48 per cent of all crimes featured in the *Hackney Gazette*'s court reports were committed by unemployed people. Many of the 'crimes' were offences that most civilised people imagine went out with Dickensian London: unemployed teenagers stealing a sixty-pence plant to take to their mother in hospital; a father illegally re-connecting his gas supply so that his children could have a bath; the unemployed Greek-Cypriot caught stealing a pair of shoes to wear; and the mother who was caught soliciting because she needed money to buy food to feed her child. We share their guilt, because we don't care enough to help the poor.

The victims of theft are seldom those who can afford it. Often they are unemployed themselves, and the loss of a DHSS giro, or the contents of a gas-meter, can be a crippling blow. Often, the only solution is to go and rob someone else. The law of the jungle prevails.

"I came home one time and went to open my door. I didn't need my keys," reflects Brian Jarvis, looking back to the doss-house where he used to live. "I walked in and realised that my telly was missing; my music-centre was missing. The room was upside down. The door had been kicked open.

"I phoned the police. I knew who'd done it straight away, 'cos there were no outside doors or windows smashed. There were four girls and one other bloke in the

141

house. I knew it must be the bloke, 'cos a girl wouldn't have been able to kick down the door of my room. But I couldn't prove nothin'.

"A couple of weeks later, his friend came round and told me that it was him – the boy in the room above me – what done it. So I planned it, and broke into him! I took everything he had. Just like he took all my belongings, I took everything off him, including the most precious thing he had – his music. You're a Christian and you love God. That's the way it was with his music. He loved it, but I took it off him. The reason I did it was because he did it to me."

Often, the poorer the victim is, the less he can afford to lose money or belongings, and – if at home when the thief comes – the more likely he is to resist theft. The more they resist, the more likely they are to get injured. For old people, even the slightest injury can prove fatal; and the shock of burglary – the sense of being violated – is something from which they often never recover.

Sadly, many young people commit crimes, not because of the financial reward that it brings, but simply for kicks – because they're bored and have got nothing better to do. Unemployment leaves young people dispirited. Long periods of it lead to a reduction in the level of social activities (through the lack of finance) and a concentration on pastimes that offer few, if any, challenges (the most obvious example being television viewing). It's amazing how many unemployed people can still manage to afford to hire or purchase a beat-up old TV; but without it, there's nothing at all for them to do all day. The only way of breaking out of the lethargy, for some of them, is through crime. The proceeds from a theft can further drive them out of lethargy, through the luxuries that are suddenly available.

"You've only got to look at the violence on TV," says my full-time colleague Nick Simpson. "*The A-Team* for example, and the other programmes that kids like. Is it any wonder the kids are the way they are with that kind of example? *Minder* too, portrays crooks as being really lovable, nice blokes. When the heroes are getting mixed up in all sorts of dubious activities, it's not surprising when the kids take after them."

The violence we see on TV is often unreal. People are involved in car crashes, or horrific battles, then get up and walk away unscathed. I believe that this puts the false idea in young people's minds that violence and crime don't really hurt people. Here are some of the comments that came out in a discussion amongst our workers and members, about TV and home videos:

"All the kids want to do at the school where I work, is to draw or write about *The A-Team*, and violence"; "I know of a group of four-year-olds who watched Michael Jackson's *Thriller* video at a kids' party"; and "We had some ten-year-olds in Junior Club tonight, talking about *Friday the 13th* and loving it. Who takes responsibility for showing them these things?"

Our local London City Missioner once tried to show cartoon films at a kids' party, but they all wanted to see something gruesome, like *Driller Killer*, or *The Texas Chainsaw Massacre*.

Following our discussion, we decided that one positive step we could take as a Christian club was to write to two local video-hire shops, pointing out that they shouldn't be loaning X-rated material to young children. We could also write to the major TV companies and film producers complaining about the effect that their programmes and films are having on young people.

I see the effects of media-violence, poverty and deplorable living conditions on the young people who come into our club. I'm often the one they come to when they're in trouble with the police.

Only recently there was a lad who was caught stealing and had to go to the local police station for an official reprimand. He was under age, so his parents were supposed to go with him; they refused, so I had to go with him instead. (It seems that he'd removed a house key from someone's pocket at school, while they were doing PT. He gave the key to one of his mates, who burgled the lad's house and returned the key before the end of the PT lesson.)

Young people often feel threatened by the police, who frequently stop them, seemingly without good cause. Common complaints are that police officers are sarcastic; they think that black people have a chip on their shoulders; they regularly harass black people; that they take young people to the police station 'on suspicion'; and that they very rarely tell young people about what their rights are when they're taken in.

I've heard it said in the club that a black person can't drive a decent car around Hackney without being stopped by the police. "Where did you nick that from then, eh?" they say. "The police judge by appearance," say our members, "but look at the Mafia. They wear suits, but they kill people!"

There are clearly a lot of bigoted coppers in the 'Met', but then there are bound to be bad people in all occupations, who give everyone else in the profession a bad name. I'm certainly grateful to the policeman who knocked me up out of bed at four in the morning the other week. "We've got your video back," he said. I didn't even know that it had been stolen! It seems that an organised gang had been going along the whole street, systematically breaking into every house.

They'd been caught because a woman walking down the street at two o'clock in the morning had spotted something suspicious and phoned for the police. That's extraordinary in itself; it's usually unheard of for a woman to be out by herself so late. Oddly enough, that very evening, I'd been leading a Bible study on "Where your treasure is, there will your heart be also." I'd said that I wasn't interested in earthly things. I wonder if I would have felt the same if the burglars had got away with my household possessions?

Crime and violence are rife in the inner-city, and there's not a lot that one can do as an individual to prevent it. As a club, attached to a church, there is an opportunity to get alongside the robber and the robbed – to dissuade the former from continuing in their ways, and to comfort the latter in their grief.

But there's a real danger of becoming obsessed with the evil and not presenting the good. There is a spirit of darkness in the world that can only be countered through Christ-like action. It's particularly severe in urban areas, and Christians living there desperately need the support of those who live outside, if we are to let the light of the world shine into the darkness of the inner-city. It's better to light one candle than to grumble against the darkness. Please light one for us now; by praying through the problems mentioned in the previous three chapters.

12

DRINK AND DRUGS

"I feel good and relaxed when I'm drinking. I don't depend on nothin' else. I think there's a God up there, but I don't believe in 'im, or depend on 'im. Know what I mean?"

Nineteen-year-old Veronica Pitman sat in my office with her friend Katie Ansell, and a few other people, discussing the whole complex issue of drink and drugs – as the young people see it.

"If I came in 'ere without a drink, I couldn't do nothin'. You 'ave to 'ave a drink to make yer laugh. Well, I 'ave a laugh at work, an' I don't drink there. I work in a fact'ry, and I get bored. I just feel 'I've got to 'ave a drink' but I can't! I don't think drink's a bad thing."

Perhaps if she was doing something more interesting, she wouldn't be bored, and wouldn't need the alcohol to knock herself out as a means of escape.

If the members smuggle drink into the club, it's usually a strong drink – Special Brew or Export. In fact, anyone seen drinking ordinary strength beer is sometimes ridiculed by the other members as being a softy. "The younger kids do it to appear macho," thinks Nick Simpson.

The white members drink in order to get drunk; it's usually a rite of passage into manhood to get absolutely sloshed a few times, and to do silly things while drunk. I remember when I was a lad, I used to pretend to be more drunk than I was, in order to 'get away' with being as uninhibited as possible. But the blacks are more 'social' drinkers. They might get high on dope more often than whites, but for them it's a prestigious matter to be able to 'take one's drink'. They therefore drink as much as anyone else, but let on that they can 'take it' because of their maturity, thinks Vernon.

Drinking is simply a means of building up self-esteem for many young people, though – of course – they would never admit that. The image of a non-drinker is neither social, nor tough; whereas the image of a drinker is quite the opposite.

We used to allow members who are eighteen or over to drink openly in the club. We did this largely because they were going to do it anyway, and going around 'policing' the club, stopping members from drinking alcohol, was taking up far too much valuable time that ought to have been spent on proper youth work. But certain members were abusing this. We felt that the time was right to stand up and say, "Because this is a Christian club, we're going to uphold Christian values". The members have a choice; if they choose to come to our club, they must obey our rules. No smoking dope, and no drinking alcohol are virtually our only rules, and we only insist that such activities don't actually take place within the club – they can drink or smoke outside and come in under the influence, if they like. We felt that we didn't want to be just an extension of the pub; we wanted to get back to being a club where education and growth can take place.

Sometimes the problem is not that the young person has a drink problem, but that the *parent* is a heavy drinker. Alcoholism can take two main forms. The first is the need to drink everyday, though the amount drunk may often not be enough to get extremely drunk – the condition is more one of alcohol dependence. The second form manifests itself as an ability to go without alcohol for several days at a time, but the moment the alcoholic begins to drink, he/she cannot stop until they are completely drunk. Either form can make life miserable for a young person living in the same household as a parent with a drink problem.

Young people who live with an alcoholic parent often think, consciously or unconsciously, that they are somehow the cause of their parent's alcoholism. The trauma often causes them to retreat into themselves, or to have a place to which they can escape when the going gets too tough.

Many alcoholic parents go out to the pub to get drunk, but some stay at home and drink in front of the television – perhaps using a sports programme as an excuse to have a few cans. Others try to hide their drinking. Common 'give-aways' that someone has an alcohol problem are: gulping drinks; drinking a lot before getting drunk; staying drunk for several days; hiding bottles in ingenious cubby-holes; talking a lot about drink; choosing friends who are also heavy drinkers; not eating much; sleeping at times when most people are awake, and getting up in the middle of the night; and having shakes or trembles.

Through not being fully aware of their surroundings, drunks may not pay much attention to the way they are dressed. Judith Seixas, in her book *How to Cope with an Alcoholic Parent*, says: "They may be partially dressed, forget to close buttons and zips, or they may be found walking around their homes without anything on at all." This, of course, can be embarrassing for young people. But it's even worse if a parent begins to make sexual advances towards them. The feelings of guilt and resentment of being used can be overpowering.

Alcoholism is an illness. The 'patient' feels sick and cannot think straight, but is generally afraid to stop drinking. They're running away from reality, or from a specific problem. They may be having work problems because the standard of their work is unacceptable, or they may have lost their job through alcoholism. At home, broken promises, embarrassment and confusion abound. Unfortunately, many young people don't realise any of this. To them, it is quite normal, say, for dad to go to the pub straight from work, and roll home at midnight singing bawdy songs.

My mate Jimmy Murphy had problems with an alcoholic father. The family's standard of living was very low, considering the amount of money which should have been going into the home from his father's job as a barber, because of the amount that he was spending on booze. As a child, Jimmy would be woken up at all hours of the night by the sound of his parents arguing, or his dad coming in noisily and fighting with his mother. "My brothers, my sister and myself would be crying. We'd hide under the bedclothes in fear, unable to understand why the two most important adults in our lives were unable to get along with each other," says Jimmy. It's a wonder that his dad didn't seriously injure someone through shaving them while his hand was trembling with DTs.

It affects girls in a very different way. Studies indicate that girls whose fathers were alcoholics often marry alcoholic men, perhaps through subconscious identification with their mothers. Many young people have fears that they will take after an alcoholic parent and become one themselves. But such worries seldom stop them from experimenting with alcohol.

The gang to which I used to belong started drinking at the age of fourteen. We'd buy bottles of cheap wine from off-licences or, better still, go back to someone's house while their parents were out. (We would only take their parents' *drink*, but, sadly, in some cultures now, it's not unusual for young junkies to get started by taking their parents' *drugs*.) The parents would often notice that the levels in the drink bottles had dropped while they were out, but we soon got wise to this and began topping the bottles up with water!

In the club we try to reason with the young people and explain the futility of using alcohol as a means of escape from life's problems. "Drinking to cover up sadness, to make yourself feel better, or to get away from problems, will only work for short periods of time," we tell them.

"Eventually you sober up and have to deal with the problem itself."

"When you smoke a joint, you don't have hallucinations, or start freaking out," explained Veronica, not that I was in any doubt. I soon progressed from alcohol onto marijuana when I was a kid. "It's just like smoking a fag," she says, but I have to disagree with her there.

"My brother's thirty-five and he's been smoking for years," she argues, as though it were some big deal. "He's not gone onto heroin, or nothin' like that. I'm nineteen now, and I've been smokin' weed since I was eleven, and I've not touched nothin' else.

"I don't feel depressed, I just feel bored. But if I hadn't just smoked a joint, I'd be depressed."

George Beschner and Kerry Treasure, in *Youth Drug Abuse,* point out that:

> As with most aspects of their lives, the drug-taking behaviour of girls (and women) has been stereotyped. Girls have been cast in a paradoxical role: on the one hand, they are viewed as having a less serious drug problem than boys; on the other hand, a girl with a drug problem is considered to be sicker than her male counterpart.

But the stereotype is not supported by findings! There is very little difference in illicit drug usage between males and females. Young women, no less than their male counterparts, are struggling to gain independence from their parents and to achieve a perception of their self-identity. To do this, they often turn to their peer-group for support, and through the peer-group can easily be ensnared by drug abuse, without their parents ever finding out.

But it's not just their peer-group from which young people can pick up bad drug habits. In some cultures, it's quite normal for parents to smoke marijuana, or 'gunja' as they sometimes call it, openly in front of their children.

Is it little wonder then, that the children want to try it for themselves? Back in the 1950s it was considered daring to smoke a cigarette when you were under age. (I remember having a packet hidden away for myself when I was still at junior school.) The sense of 'being grown-up enough to indulge' spread to alcohol in the early sixties and, by the early seventies, smoking dope had become another rite of passage into adulthood.

Many young people believe that marijuana is a *safe* drug, but it is dangerous in much the same way that alcohol is dangerous. The person under the influence of marijuana refuses to acknowledge the perception distortion, and argues that he/she functions equally well with or without the drug. There is also a minority of people whose system cannot tolerate the drug, and develop paranoid reactions under its influence. But the biggest danger, probably, is that marijuana users will soon get bored with the drug and progress onto something more potentially harmful, for their kicks. It's usually the whites who want to progress onto harder drugs. For the blacks, smoking gunja is much more enshrined in their culture (the Rastafarians take it for religious reasons, and in Jamaica it's often used as a herb – the women make tea from it) so they're less inclined to move onto anything harder.

"You're supposed to be the youth of our society, and there you are – blotto! You're not even in it. You keep opting out all the time!" I tell the users in our club, to whom drug abuse is a defence mechanism to keep anxiety at bay. I don't see any point in being gentle with them when they're on marijuana (or on the 'downers' that some of them take) since the effect of either drug is to make them so lethargic that it would take an H-bomb to shake them out of their complacency. Often, I can use their desire to get high to turn their thoughts to Jesus. "I'm on a permanent buzz," I tell them. "But I'm not opting *out*; I'm opting *in*! I know what's going on, and where I am. *Your* buzz is just an escape." But inside, I know what they're going through, from my own experience with drugs.

At home one night, during my early teens, my brother – with whom I shared a room – attacked me, saying that I had spiders crawling all over me. I didn't! I soon realised that he was hallucinating under the influence of some illicit drug. In my youthful naïvety, it all seemed very exciting – so I resolved to try drugs myself. Already my friends and I were getting drunk on cider and cheap wine every Friday night and, at fifteen, had started drinking in pubs. When I learned that I could score drugs at the old Pedro Cafe, it was just one step further into the drug culture.

It was at the time of all the gang fighting, and we'd commonly take amphetamines (powerful stimulants) before going up to take on a rival gang. The drugs would make us wild; I remember one lad being killed when two gangs started throwing spiked metal railings at one another – he was impaled. It was a step up from the days when we used to play 'chicken' by lying on railway lines when a train was coming, to get our kicks. In one of our drug-crazed revelries, we went along to a concert at the local Salvation Army hall, and beat up all the Christians!

Our gang would frequently go away for weekends of camping and drug-taking. On one occasion, we had a 'bad trip'. Our sense of direction had become so disorientated that, after a fight at a local arcade, we had difficulty in finding our way back to the tent. When we eventually succeeded, we started hallucinating; I had a remarkable experience of imagining that the tent had been turned inside out, that we were surrounded by invisible people, and that a UFO had landed nearby! I thought I'd taken Dexy's Midnight Runners (a type of amphetamine) but wonder now whether I'd been given an hallucinogen, such as LSD, instead. Many of my friends have since moved on to heroin, which is currently cheaply available in the East End, and have died. I feel lucky to be still alive and kicking. It's clear that my limited drug abuse damaged me physically in some way though; at seventeen I tried to join the Regular Army, but failed the medical.

Heroin is probably the most dangerous drug of all. Along with opium, methadone and morphine, it forms a branch of drugs known as opiate narcotics, which abusers use to escape from their troubles. Even in small doses, they can cause nausea and vomiting. Higher doses lead to insensitivity and unconsciousness; and overdoses cause comas, respiratory arrest, and death. It's a very ugly drug. Heroin-addicts, like other drug misusers, easily become cut off from ordinary life. They lose friends and move in a small circle of drug-orientated acquaintances, often turning to crime to finance their habit.

What is a youth worker to do to help such people? Our particular role in preventing drug misuse is to ensure, through suitable health education, that all young people know about the dangers of misusing drugs. Drugs can be beneficial if taken under medical supervision in the prescribed quantities but, taken to excess, they are *always harmful*. Besides explicit teaching about drugs, youth workers can help by alleviating the conditions which drive young people towards drugs. Drug abuse is a symptom of anxiety, low self-esteem and lack of confidence. By raising young people's self-esteem and confidence, we can reduce their need to resort to drugs.

In practical terms, we can do this by allowing every young person, regardless of ability, to achieve some success in club activities – this may involve taking time to discover where the young person's particular gifts lie – and by providing support in moments of uncertainty and self-doubt. Care must be taken not to over-react to situations, but rather to provide alternatives to drug abuse (for example through an exciting and varied club programme) and by giving support, counselling and protection.

Primitive man got high by inhaling intoxicating smokes and fumes. Modern youth generally prefers to sniff cocaine or other hard drugs; but glue, or other chemical solvents, are cheaper and easier to acquire. Like other inhaled drugs, the fumes have a more immediate effect than any drug taken orally, reaching the brain via the heart and lungs. 'Sniffers' abuse themselves with an amazing array of domestic substances, including nail-polish remover, lighter fuel, petrol, dry-cleaning fluid, paint thinner and, in some parts of the USA, shoe polish.

Whatever way the solvent is taken, the side-effects are horrific. According to most medical reports, these can range from a loss of appetite, nausea, vomiting, and diarrhoea, through to chest pains, ringing in the ears, muscular pains and a wide range of eye complaints. The question of whether brain damage occurs is difficult to answer. It's long been thought that the kick a solvent abuser gets is caused by brain cells actually being killed off. As it has been unkindly said: "Sniffing glue reduces IQ to the vegetable level."

The glue sniffing problem is bad enough in the East End, but it's even worse in other inner-city areas, such as Tyneside where groups of skinheads take fire extinguishers into tower blocks to sniff. They jam open lift doors, and sniff around fires that they light in the stairwells, to the grave concern of the senior citizens who live in the block. On one occasion two youths, high on glue fumes, began hurling insults at their old school, before breaking in to light a fire that caused £35,000 worth of damage.

We believe that early detection of glue-sniffing or other drug use is a key part of preventing its increase and spread. The 'early warnings' that a youth worker might be expected to detect are: declining to participate in club activities; stealing; borrowing of money from other members; disregard for physical appearance; unusual outbreaks of temper; heavy use of aftershave or perfume to disguise the smell of drugs; and wearing sunglasses at inappropriate times (to hide dilated pupils). The warning signs in groups are: stealing which appears to be the work of several individuals; talking to strangers, particularly older strangers; being the subject of rumours about drug-taking; and maintaining a distance from the other members.

Glue sniffing often meets with a negative response from professional bodies. "There is nothing we can do for you," they tell the young drug abuser. "You must stop this practice at once." But this is nothing more than a ham-fisted attempt to deal with the *symptoms* of the problem. The real problem is why the young person started sniffing glue in the first place. The first question that the youth worker has to ask is, "*Why* are you doing this?" The probable answer will be, "Because my friends do it," revealing a social need to belong to a group, and to do everything that the group does, out of a sense of insecurity.

And where has the insecurity come from? It probably derives from some lack of attention or other problem of home life – or of family life. So very often, glue sniffing – and other forms of drug abuse – are *not* youth problems, but adult problems. If the Church were able to play a more positive part in family life, family relationships could be strengthened. The real way that the Church can help with the drug problem is not by saying, "Don't do that", but simply by being more effective in its role as the salt and light of the world. Youth work alone seldom opens up enough opportunities to deal adequately with a whole family, so all we can do is to warn of the dangers, and to help the young people to build their security on something else – ideally on Jesus, but possibly, in the short term, on some sense of their own worth.

13
RACISM AND SEXISM

> In Samaria Jesus came to a town named Sychar, which was
> not far from the field that Jacob had given to his son Joseph.
> Jacob's well was there, and Jesus, tired out by the journey,
> sat by the well. It was about noon.
>
> A Samaritan woman came to draw some water, and
> Jesus said to her, "Give me a drink of water."
>
> The woman answered, "You are a Jew and I am a
> Samaritan – so how can you ask me for a drink?"
>
> Jesus answered, "If only you knew what God gives and
> who it is that is asking you for a drink, you would ask him,
> and he would give you life-giving water." (John 4:5–10
> GNB)

This is a very familiar passage of Scripture that we've
probably all read many times. But, in becoming familiar
with it, we have, I suggest, *overspiritualised* it.

A Jew reading the passage would have been struck by
the importance of the location, with its appeal to
tradition and culture. But, more forcefully, the original
Jewish readers would have been flabbergasted that Jesus
should speak to either a Samaritan or a woman. That he
should have spoken to someone who was not only a
female Samaritan, but who was 'living in sin' with a man
to whom she was not married, must have seemed like the
last straw!

In the Middle East, in Christ's day, woman was
regarded as little more than property to be sold by a
father and bought by her husband. She was a 'non-
person' unworthy of respect or esteem in her own right.
The Samaritans were a race apart, despised by the Jews.
The passage, therefore, is a profound comment on the

twin evils of sexism and racism. Christ, by simply talking to the Samaritan woman, was defying all the social taboos of the day; his reaction to the prejudices and bigotries laid upon him was simply to ignore them! Surely, as followers of Christ, we too have a duty to oppose bias and unreasoning hatred wherever they may be found. In today's society, and particularly for young people in inner-city areas, they take many forms.

A paper on *Ethnic Minority Youth Employment*, presented to government by the Commission for Racial Equality in 1980, shows that ethnic minorities are disproportionately represented amongst the unemployed, especially during a recession. In other words, young blacks are discriminated against. Between November 1973 and November 1977, while national unemployment doubled, unemployment figures for ethnic minorities quadrupled. Department of Employment statistics from February 1979 to February 1980, show that again black unemployment rose *four times faster than overall unemployment!* Ethnic minority unemployment is particularly severe amongst the unskilled. By and large, young blacks are at the bottom of the pile, with the chips so strongly stacked against them that they are unable to move from such a position. In conclusion, the report carries the grim warning: "Failing the development of a constructive initiative, future prospects are bleak – a whole lost generation of untrained and unemployed young people. They have already shown that they will not be a silent or passive generation."

The only real solution to the problems of mass unemployment and disproportionate unemployment, I feel, has to come from central government through the creation of *genuine* new jobs. The best that youth work can do is to fight a 'containing operation', to prevent the feelings of unrest and bitterness from breaking out onto the streets – as it has occasionally done in Brixton, Toxteth, Handsworth and Tottenham, where the double disadvantage of being both unemployed and black easily fan the spark of discontent to an all-consuming flame.

Though numerically strong in inner-London, (in Brent, Hackney and Haringey, one-third of all births are to women from the Commonwealth, compared with a national average of 6 per cent) I find that blacks have a low sense of personal worth. The black peoples are held captive by the bars and chains of white social convention.

One of the worst of those conventions, I believe, is to assume that all black people are the same. In fact, the black population of Britain is an amalgamation of three cultures that are vastly different from one another: the Africans, the West Indians, and the Asians. Even that is a bland understatement. Africans from different countries have vastly different cultures and, even within the same country, there are enormous differences between regions.

In West Indian culture, many sociologists say, the family structure is different from the norm for white Europeans. Between 60 per cent and 80 per cent of live births are recorded as illegitimate, but that is not to say that they are mainly to single-parent families. To the contrary, these births take place into caring, loving relationships which simply have not been consecrated by marriage vows. It is an established part of their culture for two people to live together out of wedlock. (In parts of Jamaica, in up to two-thirds of all families, the parents are married only in 'common law'.) I'm told that, sociologically, the flexible, open family loyalties and ties are no less stable than a conventional Western marriage.

The Asian culture too, is different from that of the West. There is a greater emphasis on family honour, which takes the form of not being indebted – say, to the State for social security hand-outs – or allowing an offence to another family member to go unpunished. I heard once of an Asian restaurant-owner who flew home to India to 'avenge the death of his brother'! In Asian culture, the role of the woman is significantly lower even than in sexist European society. Oddly, in Asian culture, one finds a greater affinity to the New Testament picture of an extended family, having everything in common, than anything that the Western Church has managed to achieve. In India, there is a strong caste system which perpetuates itself – to a greater or lesser degree – in Britain, amongst the Asian immigrant population.

To understand where young Africans are 'coming from', we need briefly to look at their history of living in Britain. The earliest Africans arrived as slaves, 'imported' from West Africa in the eighteenth century. Later immigrants, though coming of their own free will, were leaving Commonwealth countries that had been badly exploited by British imperialism in the nineteenth century. Is it really any wonder that they feel oppressed by whites? For nearly three hundred years, they've been getting a rough deal. They *feel* oppressed because they *are* oppressed! Alex Haley's semi-autobiographical book and TV series *Roots* has documented white oppression, with all its horrors. A joke going the rounds in the early eighties went: "I see that they're showing *Roots* on TV again. This time, they're running it backwards so that it'll have a happy ending!"

The Church did a good job in helping to liberate the black people from slavery, largely through the efforts of nineteenth-century social reformers like Lord Shaftesbury. But the good work has largely been undone by the widespread intolerance of black people in recent years.

When half a million West Indians arrived in Britain in the fifties and sixties, their high level of church attendance (as high as 69 per cent in one survey) contrasted with the low percentage of white church-goers in the same areas; the West Indians settled mainly in inner-city areas where regular church attendance was around one per cent. I find that some of the immigrants have reacted strongly against both the the cold 'formal' styles of worship, and the hostile reception that they received from the WASPs – White Anglo-Saxon Protestants. How the absurdity of racial prejudice strikes home when one realises that even we so-called 'native' Englishmen are actually a curious mish-mash of Ancient Britons, Celts, Picts, Romans, Anglo-Saxons, and

Norman conquerers!).

John Rex, in his article in the book *Black Youth in Crisis*, notes that orthodox Anglicanism or Methodism does not meet the cultural, social or spiritual needs of the black community, and that the Pentecostal or Holiness churches command a commitment and a loyalty far greater amongst their members, and may well have a greater long-term influence. As John Rex says:

> To go to a meeting of West Indian pastors from the Independent Churches, is to enter a world of working-class religion which has largely disappeared amongst the native working class. There is a simple atmosphere of faith, a joy of communion and community, an unaffected enjoyment of singing and worship and a belief, above all, in the spontaneous and immediate action of the Holy Spirit rather than a sacramental grace dispensed solely by ordained priests. To discover the fellowship of a West Indian congregation is to discover a kind of release and happiness which the mundane world of work does not allow.

One of our neighbouring churches, The Risen Christ and All Souls on Clapton Park estate, had a problem with its black membership, in that it could attract black women, but not black men. I don't know whether there was some feature of their services or mid-week meetings which was putting men off, but the problem persisted for several years until – largely through prayer – the male blacks started coming. It's sad though that most of the black Christians in the borough attend churches that are 100 per cent black. It doesn't do much to help the Church's stand against racism to have voluntary segregation between churches. The all-black churches seem to be meeting particular needs at the present, but I can't think that the situation can be anything but short-term, until the Church in Hackney can become fully racially integrated.

It must be strange growing up as a black Christian in a white-dominated society, with all the pictures of Jesus in story books showing him as a blue-eyed WASP, when he was actually of multi-racial Semitic stock, his skin much darker than that of Europeans. It seems that we WASPs have re-made Christ in our own image.

Current research suggests that black youngsters are more likely to be 'at risk' than white youths; but the definition of 'at risk' is a white one! The research is 'loaded' by white preconceptions of what is 'normal' in society. For example, Mr Anthony Steen (a past member of the Select Committee on Race Relations and Immigration) identifies the 'problem' of West Indian child care in these terms: "The West Indian cultural pattern fails to perceive the benefit which accrues from playing and talking with children." But this is a *judgement* on West Indian culture made from a jaundiced white viewpoint.

Anthropologist Edith Clarke's study of Jamaica concludes that the mother "depends on even very young children to fetch and carry for her. Whatever she may be doing in the yard, the children are never far away. There is a constant companionship, and a constant inter-dependence."

It's clear then, that West Indian women express their love and concern for their children, not in a *lesser* way, but simply in a *different* way. In fact, since the West Indian way is less passive (and, incidentally, closer to the culture of the Bible) it is arguably *better* than the European way.

Education is, we believe at St Paul's club, another area of unfair discrimination. ILEA figures suggest that black youngsters who were born and fully educated in Britain were functioning at a much lower level than their white classmates. The performance of West Indian children, at the age of eleven, after six years of primary schooling, was such that only 8 per cent, instead of an expected 25 per cent, were in the top band.

At many secondary schools, outside London (and in London in the past) all the children get taught about

161

white history – which makes out that only European culture is of any importance. Blacks are portrayed as savages who were living in mud huts until the noble white man arrived! It would be fairer if blacks and whites were taught the histories of the black peoples, as well as European history. This apparently was tried during the seventies but failed. It was one thing to try to change schoolchildren's ideas, but quite another to try to change those of the teachers! Altering the curriculum achieved very little, because the thinking of the schools remained unchanged; and the broader problems remained untouched. There is also considered to be a danger that, if too successful, the approach could create a sense of identity – and hence, solidarity – amongst the black schoolchildren, which could have a polarising effect. But the more progressive Educational Authorities (i.e. ILEA) are now aware of the problems, and actively moving towards solutions.

The worst form of discrimination is probably the pure, irrational bigotry which leads to violence. During a discussion at St Paul's club, in the course of which we tried to find reasons behind racial hatred, it was suggested that white people are actually physically scared of black people. They know that black people stick together more than whites. If a white guy was being beaten up by blacks, most of the members felt that other white guys would not join in; but if it was a black guy being attacked by whites, it was felt that other blacks would intervene – regardless of the right or wrong of the situation. If I saw either incident, I would feel that I had to stop the fight, and find out how the incident had started – but it seems that, in Hackney, I would be in a minority.

Vernon, our black part-time worker, has never felt in any real danger of racial violence within the club, probably due to our racially-integrated membership (I wish that churches could be as integrated.) Many of the young people of different races have grown up alongside one another so, to them, it's natural to be friends with people with different coloured skin.

The closest that Vernon has come to trouble was late one night, on his way to a party: "I wasn't really sure where the party was, so I kept stopping and looking around. A police car stopped, and three uniformed officers got out and quizzed me about what I was doing. Once I'd convinced them that I was on the level, they even helped me to try to find the place. After I left them, I saw a Cortina with five white blokes in it. It slowed down, and I was sure it was going to stop and that there'd be trouble. But, at that moment, I heard the music from the party. I walked towards it and came upon the party, so the trouble never materialised. That's the only time that I've really felt threatened because of my colour."

Though there are ripples of racism in Homerton, it's not the massive problem that it is in other parts of Hackney, or in other London boroughs. During the Brixton riots, all the owners of shops in Mare Street were evidently very worried that the violence and looting would spread to the East End, because they started boarding up the windows.

In the club, there were a number of black members who said, "We're black and we're hard done by. We're going to go and join in the rioting!" But, when I talked with them about their feelings, it became clear that – though many echoed the feelings of oppression – for some, their real interest lay in the looting that was taking place.

The riots in Toxteth (Liverpool), Handsworth (Birmingham), St Paul's (Bristol) and Highfields (Leicester) indicate that the situation is not just confined to certain London inner-city areas like Tottenham, Lewisham and Brixton. The causes, tensions and aggressions which lead to the rioting are startlingly similar to those found elsewhere in Hackney – particularly in Stoke Newington.

Though the violence has not flared up to any significant extent in Hackney yet, all the necessary factors are present except that the poverty, the unemployment, the bad housing conditions and the lack of self-esteem are probably much more acute problems in Hackney than in the areas that have actually seen trouble. We've been fortunate so far, but I wonder if it's just a matter of time before some incident in the borough triggers what is likely to be the *worst* rioting we have yet seen.

Mary Fuller, in her article in *Black Youth in Crisis,* points out that black women are doubly subordinated, by both sexual and racial repression. Analysis of these twin repressions is often carried out in parallel, rather than in tandem, says Mary. Consequently, she believes, little is really known about the double repression, except that black women form a discernible subculture.

Many black women come to believe that they genuinely *are* inferior; and this belief gives rise to self-hate, and low self-esteem. But recent work suggests that the two areas may have contradictory – and not cumulative – effects. The double oppression makes many black women more determined to succeed than their male or white counterparts. They are often interested in getting good jobs, to a much greater degree than their contemporaries.

Black girls find it easier to get jobs than black men. This may, perhaps, be due to the importance that black women seem to give to educational achievement. In Mary Fuller's survey, a group of black girls achieved an average of 7.6 passes at 'O' level and CSE, compared with an average of 5.6 passes by a comparative group of black boys. I think that the dream of 'a good education' has a particular significance to the black peoples, because of the myth that "they are only oppressed because they are ignorant".

Black girls at St Paul's club often express considerable resentment that their brothers are not expected to undertake domestic tasks either at all, or to the same extent, as themselves. But these tasks often contribute to the black girl's self-confidence, as she rationalises that her brothers are *less competent* at doing such tasks. I've heard of some sociologists who suggest that the sexual division of labour and responsibility "locks women more strongly and permanently into family responsibilities than it does men".

Women and girls have been repressed all through history. When I was at college, I wrote a thesis about women's struggle for recognition in Britain, from 1850 to 1918. The long working hours, poor health care, lack of acceptance in the professions, and the general lack of education during those years prevented most women from having any real say in their lives. Many people think that it was the suffragettes, or the less well-known Chartists, whose campaigning was primarily responsible for women being given the vote – but it's actually Kaiser Wilhelm whom they should be thanking!

During the First World War, when the cream of the male population was sent off to the fronts, they were paid so badly that women had to go out to work to help to keep their families. With so many men being away, they were able to step into much more responsible jobs. Through helping to keep the munitions industry going, women were able to *prove* themselves the equal of men in a way that had never before been possible.

Since those days, the Second World War has given women further opportunities to show their abilities. Increased affluence, the development of the welfare state, and the provision of state schooling have reduced the need for teenaged girls to go out to work to help to support the family, and have opened up better education and greater career prospects for young women. But still, an irrational fear and discrimination exists against women.

Women are badly treated just because they are female. Men don't seem to take into account the way that girls feel. If you are a lad in a youth club, and you want to do something, you go ahead and do it. But when a girl comes in, unless she's quite confident, she won't – for example – put ten pence down and wait in the queue to play pool. Girls don't normally do that. The girls come in and sit around, but they don't usually get involved.

When girl meets boy, boy *dominates* girl. I don't think it happens consciously, but it's a fact of life! I think it'll always go on while, in competition terms, women find it hard to compete with men – or are uninterested in competing. In education terms, I believe that men could do a lot more to make women feel more comfortable in a youth club, school or work situation. I always say to the lads: "Look, you have to remember that girls aren't the same as boys! It sounds silly, but remember that a girl isn't going *to push*. She's not out to 'put one over on you'." I try to get to the male ego, and try to convince the guys that there's no need to feel threatened if a girl beats him at pool.

"There was a girl in the office where I used to work," says Vernon, "She was a really good mate. She was a tom-boy, and she'd go down to the pub with the lads. I wouldn't mind being beaten at pool by her." But, to the others she was no longer a girl. She'd become a boy, through playing a male role. And, when a girl plays a boy's role, the lads don't mind being beaten by her – because she's lost her femininity. It's the idea that femininity is the equal of masculinity that frightens most young males. It's the idea of the feminine girl that they can't cope with. When a feminine girl comes along, they have to reduce her to a sex object, in order to protect their own egos.

In the film *Gregory's Girl*, Gregory – a spotty, adolescent teenager – becomes infatuated with a girl who is able to compete with males at football. But his classmates fail to see the attraction; "She's just a girl," they say. They can't accept that she can be good at football *and* retain her femininity. To them, any footballing skills she has must serve to reduce her sexual desirability, and vice-versa. At the end of the film, the contradictions become too much for Gregory too, and he goes out with a less-threatening girl. It's an archetypal story. None of the lads at St Paul's club would long pursue a girl who, say, constantly beat him at pool. His ego would never stand it.

Sexism is primarily a male problem, but it's so difficult to re-educate lads in their thinking towards girls, that any youth worker involvement in the situation is usually directed at helping the girls to cope with male prejudices. One such project which does this is the Camden Unemployed Young Women's Project.

This is a series of courses for unemployed girls, who are perceived as having different needs from men or older women. "The job market is very clearly sex stereotyped," says their 1982 report. "The highest paid jobs and most powerful jobs have historically been reserved for men." High unemployment has generated a condition where young women – whose working lives are often treated as nothing more than a prelude to marriage – are discouraged from taking jobs away from men, who are still traditionally regarded as the bread-winners.

The courses are intended to promote the young women's feelings of success and achievement, through sessions concentrating on educational, personal and career development. Like all other forms of youth work, its aim is *growth* – in self-esteem, development of personal skills, and ability to relate to other people. It equips them to overcome any inferiority that they may feel as females. It is a laudable project, and shames the Church for not taking on something along similar lines. At St Paul's, we'd like to try to emulate its enterprising and unthreatening approach, when we have the resources to offer facilities for unemployed young women ourselves. We need to cut through the barriers of sexism and racism, if we are to enable Christ to give his life-giving water to a thirsty world.

14

SEX AND MORALITY

I can vividly remember my first sexual encounter. It was embarrassing! I was a seventeen-year-old skinhead, talking to a mate's girlfriend in a pub; we were waiting for my mate to come in. I don't know if it was just the drink, or whether she'd had her eye on me for a while, but – as the evening grew late, and my mate had still not arrived – she moved nearer to me. In all sorts of non-verbal ways she seemed to be saying that she fancied me. I was flattered!

We ended up in the back of a car on Hackney Downs. It's not the most private place, even with the windows steamed up. Like most young people, I knew a thing or two about sex from biology lessons and playground gossip, but that kind of education ill-prepared me for actual sexual intimacy. I was scared! I didn't really know what I was supposed to do, or what was expected of me. Sex is messy! I don't think anyone is very good during their first tentative exploration.

We didn't go 'all the way', but I was still walking around in trepidation the next day. What if I hadn't been any good, and the girl had told everyone? And what would my mate say when he found out what I'd been up to with his girlfriend? I fully expected the incident to result in a fight, but my mate wasn't very concerned. His only regret was that I hadn't waited for him, so that he could have joined in a 'gang bang'.

Though that happened back in the sixties, I doubt if the situation was any different from the sexual encounters which take place in Hackney in the eighties. Though once it was the teenaged lad who was expected to make all the moves, girls are now becoming much more forthright in making a play for a bloke they like. I watched a TV documentary recently, where a teenaged girl made the comment: 'You have to chase your man or you'll never get anywhere. But the men don't like it. It's taking away their role, their ego, their masculinity.'' I think that a lot of guys pretend that they've made the first move – even to themselves – when it's been the girl who was making the running all the time.

Girls, traditionally, had a 'star' system as to how far they let a boy 'go' with them – one star for a kiss, two for a hand on the knee, etc. But girls today are expected to go 'all the way' from the very beginning. Virginity is not fashionable in the inner-city; it's almost regarded as some sort of disease, to be gotten-rid-of as soon as possible. A male on the same TV documentary emphasised the expectations that a teenaged boy feels placed upon him: "For a teenaged boy, losing your virginity is the most important thing in the world. On the other hand, it's the most terrifying thing, because you don't know what's going to happen." I can identify strongly with that sentiment.

Once a girl has lost her virginity – once that barrier has been crossed – she becomes less concerned about whom she sleeps with; this leads easily to promiscuity, and she may not be able to cope with the pressures that this brings, at an early age. She's more likely to be able to cope with sexual relations if she keeps her virginity until her wedding night. But there is a tremendous pressure for a girl to sleep with a boy, in Hackney. "If I *go* with him people may say that I'm a slag; but if I don't, I'll lose him," they say.

Sexual relationships involve a whole series of double standards, in which the girl loses out. If a boy sleeps around, or mistreats his girl, he's 'sowing his wild oats,' or 'being a bit of a lad', any euphemism except the correct one – that he's 'sinning'. But a girl who sleeps around – often because she is desperate for real affection – soon becomes known as 'an easy lay' or a 'slut'. An even bigger piece of hypocrisy is that the lads all expect the girl they eventually marry to be a virgin!

A lot of these sexual attitudes, and the problems that they bring, have their origins in the young peoples' home lives and upbringing. In a healthy family, children receive plenty of physical contact in the form of caresses and cuddling, which convey good feelings. In the first year of life, the sense of being loved is intimately linked with physical closeness; and throughout childhood, physical touch is a powerful sensation. But, in many homes, the only physical contact the child receives is through being shaken, hit, dropped, or tossed across the room. In some instances, the child sees the same treatment being inflicted on their mother, by their father. A child learns so much from observing parental behaviour, that it's far from surprising when young females expect to be badly treated by their boy friends, who are afraid of being thought 'sissy' if they aren't aggressive, or if they don't knock their girls about.

One of the girls at our club sleeps around because she's seen her mother do it. Naturally, we try to discourage this sort of behaviour at St Paul's club; but we have to be careful not to be seen to be prohibiting it as though it were the enforcement of just another rule. Rather, we try to talk through and reason out the causes with the young people. Our job is not simply to protect the innocent, but to rehabilitate the 'guilty'.

When a young person reaches puberty, the fact that menstruation is connected with ovulation, or that semen is loaded with sperm, are not matters with which young adolescents are concerned. Much more important to them are the changing shape of their bodies, the growth of hair in comical places, and the fact that genital stimulation brings erotic pleasure. To expect a young person to consider the ethics of sexual behaviour at that juncture is absurd. Factors such as insecurity, fear, anxiety and uncertainty cloud and colour any real thinking about such issues. Here, if a youth worker is consulted, any anxiety must be met with reassurance, and any guilt with appropriate explanation. Often at this stage, the goodness of sex becomes sullied by sexual experimentation and mutual masturbation. This creates much greater problems for the Christian youth worker.

I believe that young people have sex simply as an experiment, to see what it is like. With the males, it's also responsible for their status: the more girls you've slept with, the more of a man you are. Bragging to your mates afterwards is an important part of the sex game – and a game is all it is for many young eastenders. If you didn't get very far with your girl last night, then you make something up rather than risk ridicule – I'm sure that many more conquests are claimed than are ever made. Feelings and love do not enter into the situation. Their motto is: "If it feels good, do it." But they don't know what psychological damage is being done to them by this attitude. They don't know *any* of the risks that they are taking.

Contraception is not something which the young people think about very much. The bloke will usually assume that the girl is on the pill. He's too shy to ask her, even though he's not too shy to have sexual intercourse with her – it's part of the basic ignorance that young people have about each other's sexual functions. I remember one trip away, one girl was very embarrassed when she dropped her handbag and a sanitary napkin fell out. A lad behind her, who regards himself as something of a local stud, asked her what it was – he'd never seen one before. Both sexes are usually too embarrassed to admit that they know next to nothing about sex, apart from how to perform the act itself.

After a couple of weeks of being together and having sex, perhaps the boy may ask the girl if she's on the pill and – if not – tell her to see to it. His sexist attitudes manifest themselves in his belief that it's the woman's responsibility. "If you don't want to get pregnant, you should be on something," they say. Sadly, the girl usually obliges. There's no love or respect present.

We need to convince young people that it is *people*, and

171

not just bodies, that encounter one another during sexual activity. If pornography plays a part in a young person's life, then they need to be reminded that pornographic pictures are a distortion of real people, and that real women are much more fascinating and complex than the exaggerated pictures they see of naked flesh. Sex education in schools is all about the technicalities – it's to do with anatomical drawings – and the idea of relationships rarely enters into it. I feel that good humour, tact and honesty are the best ways of bringing young people away from an unrealistic view of sex, and setting them in a state of mind where they can begin to consider the ethics and morality of sexual behaviour.

Young men and women have an urgent *need* to be together; they want to feel that they *matter* to someone else. If this desire can be channelled into conventional Christianity, then the young person might begin to feel that, *because they matter to God*, they don't need this kind of importance in relationships with the opposite sex. But often, normal human desires being what they are, young people want to feel that they matter to a member of the opposite sex. The mistake occurs when they come to believe that they will only matter if their partner expresses affection in sexual terms. To put it bluntly, some guys will only believe that a girl cares for him if she will have sexual intercourse, and frequently, submit to sexual perversions with him.

"Marriage? What do I want with a bit of paper?" said one of our girl members, in a recent discussion. It's not an uncommon view but, let's be frank, the people who voice this view usually have a vested interest; they are almost entirely those people who have decided that they will live with a member of the opposite sex (or, today, it is sometimes a member of the same sex) and engage in full sexual relations, living in every way as though they were legally man and wife. We easily forget, of course, that legally they *are* man and wife – in common law. Common law should not be thought inferior to statute law, by which couples are normally legally married in Britain; all the marriages in the Bible are marriages under the principle of common law!

"You can live with someone for years, and then split up, and you won't have to worry about going to court and sorting out who gets what, and who's going to have the kids, or whatever," she continued. That's an interesting statement coming from a girl, who would automatically receive custody of the children, while the father would have no rights in the matter whatsoever. Sharing out the property and other joint belongings would be a much more complex process than she seems to think, though. A common-law marriage often ends with greater ill-feeling and acrimony than a normal one.

"I'm going to do what I want, not what anyone else wants me to do," she said, selfishly.

But what about love? Where is the basis of any living arrangements?

"If you love someone, you can just go and live with them. There's no guarantee that you're going to love them for the rest of your life."

No, but if you don't have the commitment of a formal marriage, there's no incentive to 'make a go of it' when the going gets rough. That's the second disadvantage of a common-law marriage. As the song says: "When the going gets tough, the tough get going." Love without commitment is a pale shadow of the genuine article.

On the one hand, I find it hard not to admire the integrity of those who refuse to submit to some *procedure* or *ceremony* in which they do not believe. On the other hand, there is still an element of hypocrisy here.

In giving themselves the tag of 'living together', instead of 'being married', they are simply conforming to current social convention. They may think of themselves as enlightened radicals but, within their own social class and peer group, they have become boringly conventional. If they *really* considered conventional marriage to be unnecessary and outmoded, then why enter into a pseudo-marriage with all the outward trappings of the real thing? It's intellectually and morally dishonest.

This, of course, supposes that marriage is simply a legal formality with no spiritual significance. Those who live together out of wedlock seldom have any kind of spiritual life, but – even for those who are married – it must be debatable whether any married couple not professing to be Christians can truly be married in the sight of God anyway, when they refuse to allow God to have any other part in their lives. Even if they sincerely wanted God to be with them on their wedding day, it must be doubtful, firstly, whether God *would* respond to such a conditional invitation; and secondly, whether God *could* be present in any real sense within the relationship between two unconfessed and unrepentant fallen humans. The tenor of Scripture suggests that God can never be so inconsistent, that he is "the same yesterday, today, forever", not present at a wedding and absent by the honeymoon.

For many young people, a church marriage service is nothing more than an excuse for a family get-together; and the building itself is wanted by the couple purely as a backdrop for the wedding photographs. For a church, and a minister of God, to be *used* in this way is – I believe – excusable only for the evangelistic opportunity to preach to a congregation many of whom enter a church only a handful of times in their lives. It is the non-Christian couple who abuse the church and God in this way, and who make solemn vows which they may not even fully understand, for whom I feel concern. That is why I believe that 'living together' can actually be, for many non-believers, the lesser of two evils. But a registry office wedding would be the better option.

Those who live together out of wedlock often do so for selfish reasons: they don't want to be alone; they wish to enjoy sexual relations without commitment; they want to 'mean something to someone else'; and they want someone to iron their shirts for them! (But, sadly, many people who marry do so for those self-same reasons . . .)

174

It isn't common-law relationships that are the problem. It's promiscuity.

"Doesn't fidelity mean anything to you?" I asked Veronica.

"Fidelity? What does that word mean?" she replied. It just didn't exist in her vocabulary.

She's currently going out with a black lad, but she's afraid to take him home to meet her mother, who holds racist views, and who certainly wouldn't approve. She couldn't take him home at the moment anyway, because he's 'inside' on remand, with armed robbery and a series of other charges against him.

"How do you know that you're in love with him?" I asked.

"Because I've stuck by him while he's been on remand. He's not even sentenced yet, and he's been inside for nine months. If I wasn't in love with him, I wouldn't write to him, I wouldn't go to see him. He's cool."

That sounded a convincing reason, until I asked her again why she remained faithful to him.

"Because," she replied, "if I went off with another bloke, and he found out, he'd kick me 'ead in!" It seemed a very strange type of love in which fear played such a large part.

"They've got a blackmail charge on him," she offered. "Now they're threatening to do 'im for assaulting a police officer. Once they've got you in for something, they try to pin more charges on you; something you've not even done. He didn't assault a police officer, they assaulted him; five of them." But it could be a sack of potatoes she's describing for all the love and concern that she showed. "They held him down and kicked the shit out of him."

Like so many young people these days, Veronica is desperate for love, but doesn't really understand what the word means. How could she? Her father left her mother with four children to go and live with another woman. And Veronica bears the emotional scars, which

175

drive her into drug abuse, and into the arms of anyone who will show her any attention. I asked her how she would feel if she decided to have children, while she wasn't married to the father.

"You don't have to be married to have children!" she exclaimed. But that's something that millions of unmarried mothers have discovered, to their cost.

"It's wrong for a man to stay with a woman just because of kids," she says, defending her own father's actions as though they were right and honourable. "I've never had me dad live with me. My mum brought us up on 'er own." It's not uncommon in the inner-city for the mistakes of the parents to repeat themselves in the children, who know no better and think it a normal way of life.

We've had quite a number of unmarried mothers through our doors over the years. It's sad to see them, and hard for us too. If we installed a contraceptive machine in one of our toilets, then perhaps one or two of them could have been prevented. But, like our stand on drink and drugs in the club, we feel that it would be wrong to compromise the Christian nature of the club in that way.

During our staff discussions, we discovered that only one of us has ever had any cause to counsel members about VD. I find it hard to believe that the problem should be so limited, in view of the promiscuity of club members. Perhaps they don't want to talk about the problem, because it confounds their belief that it's alright to have sex as often as they like, with as many different partners as possible. VD is one bad consequence of that attitude that they find impossible to ignore!

We haven't had anyone come up and admit to being gay, either. In discussion, we considered that the lads would be too afraid of abuse from their friends to adopt such an orientation. It's just not 'macho' enough to be accepted in Homerton.

But how does a youth worker go about relating Christian

176

moral values to young people, without sounding totally irrelevant to the situation? How do we make the Word incarnate in the inner-city? How can Christian values be brought to bear on everyday situations?

The only way is by a Christian worker actually *living out* those values. That applies not just to values connected with sexual relations, but also those concerned with homelessness, unemployment, family life, racism, sexism, crime, violence, drugs, and all the other issues facing young people – issues which are invariably interrelated anyway. We can't simply say to young people, "You mustn't do that because Jesus says so." That would only result in laughter and derision. Our beliefs have to be reflected in our lives, before they can be expressed verbally to young people. There's no other way.

A youth worker has power in the lives of young people, but if he/she uses it to belittle them, then that's wrong. But it's also wrong if we *permit* young people to be oppressed – while turning a blind eye – when it is within our power to change the situation.

We have to be Christ-like in our relations with young people. That means that, on occasions, it will be necessary to metaphorically 'throw the money changers out of the temple', showing righteous anger about issues that God is angry about. If, for example, we find someone peddling drugs in the club, though we might not ban that person outright, we would make it quite clear that we don't tolerate such activity, and probably tell the person not to come into the club for the next few days.

Society is becoming polarised into the 'haves' and the 'have-nots'. Inequalities and injustices are occurring which are contrary to the biblical ideal. God says, in Deuteronomy 15:4–5, that, "Not one of your people will be poor if you obey me." But the poverty of the inner-city testifies to man's basically sinful nature. Christ knew that sin would cause those inequalities to persist when he said, "You will always have poor people with you." (Mark 14:7)

But Christ also prophesied that Peter would betray

177

him – even though that was not an ideal situation – knowing that the action would lead to remorse, and that remorse would drive Peter back onto the right path for his life. We too need to feel remorse for allowing inequality to occur, and our remorse has to be clear to the young people if we are to demonstrate that poverty – and the other social evils of the inner-city – are *wrong*.

We too easily forget how influenced young people are by our actions. If we show them love, then they will learn love instead of hatred. If we give them hope, then they'll see that the world is a beautiful place. Where hope and love are present, it's possible for faith to grow.

I often hear young people say, "When I've given up drugs… when I've stopped sleeping with my girl… when I've stopped hurting people… then I'll think about God." Or they say, "I'm not good enough to be a Christian; I'd never be able to keep it up." We have to get through to young people that there is nothing *to* keep up – that we become right *by knowing God*, not by becoming 'good enough'.

Often it's necessary to counter worldly values with solid reasoning, before the Christian values can be presented. When, for example, someone says, "There's nothing wrong with sleeping around," I counter this view by talking about unwanted pregnancies, and sexually-transmitted diseases which are much more common amongst the promiscuous. I tell them that, "The more partners you have, the more likely you are to forget what love is; and to come to the mistaken belief that love and sex are the same.

"While you're under the influence of drugs, or in bondage to sex," I tell them, "you are not in your right mind. And while you're not in your right mind, you're not in control.

"Being human is about being in control of yourself; of doing what you do because you *choose* to do it. If you're under the influence of drink, drugs or sex, or if you have a violent nature, or a racist disposition, then you're a slave to that attitude. You're not a free person. *You've chained yourself up!*"

It takes months, or even years, successfully to communicate Christian moral standards to young people in a way that will 'stick'. It's taken a long time to overcome the popular belief in 'free love' which so dominated the social climate of the sixties and seventies, but the tide is turning. It's suddenly trendy again, so the tabloids tell us, to be a virgin till your wedding night. Those who give away their bodies too freely, soon feel like children who have given away the most special toy they ever owned, because they didn't know how to use it properly. The children of the eighties are disillusioned with the permissive values of the sixties. Experience is showing that marriage creates the only stable environment in which to bring up a family.

No, marriage – in the full meaning of the word, with all the stable values which it represents – is not unnecessary or outmoded. I think it's going to make the biggest comeback since Jesus Christ on Easter morning.

15

CHURCH IN THE CITY

It's very difficult to assess our success as a club. To say that young people in Homerton behave the way they do because of the influence of St Paul's club, is a statement that's impossible to prove.

There are certain achievements of which we can be sure, however. One is that the club was largely responsible for the break-up of the Kingsmead gang – one of the toughest street gangs that the East End has ever known. We achieved it through the leaders – people like Jimmy Murphy – coming to know Jesus. Without leadership, the gang was directionless, and folded up.

There are certain individuals who became Christians through the ministry of the club – my co-worker, Nick Simpson, and his brother Doug for example. But success can't adequately be measured in numerical terms. For instance, one night recently, the number of members in the club were outnumbered by the workers! I felt a failure. But the low turnout meant that I could go and see someone on church business, and I ended up in a very long counselling session. The low turnout meant that I could be a blessing to someone else in the church.

Clearly, one of the developments with which we are most pleased is the way that the old St Paul's church hall is developing into a fully-fledged community centre. But it was very much a *church* achievement, rather than a club effort. It's remarkable that such a small, impoverished inner-city church could 'get its acts together' enough to pull it off. But then, our church has a history of social action, orientated towards establishing a community centre for the Kingsmead estate. Back in the seventies, the Church was able to bring about the formation of a Tenants Association (TA). This was done partly as a means of establishing an evangelistic spearhead on Kingsmead, but largely in response to a desire to try to do something about the many hardships faced by tenants on the estate. In 1976, through the church's help, the Kingsmead TA succeeded in having a proper community centre built on the estate – and the church was able to secure a room for its exclusive use, and the facilities of the centre's main hall for Sunday services, where worship was held for Christians who were actively ministering on the estate.

Our church was one of the leading lights behind the Hackney Marshes Fun Festival, a community festival for the people of the area, which did much to break down the walls of isolation and re-establish the community spirit. Many individuals in the church have been responsible for improving the living conditions in the area. Jack Shepherd, one of our members, was for a long time the secretary of Kingsmead TA, weaning it through its developing years. There's an ILEA-run children's adventure playground just behind St Barnabas church which I was largely responsible for developing in the period immediately before I rejoined the youth project. John Pearce, our vicar, has been the instigator of more good works in the area than either of us can remember – the Homerton Space Project amongst them.

The church is firmly established, not just as the instigators of our youth project, but as a continuing supporter. Our management committee is technically a sub-committee of its PCC, from which we derive our charitable status. Our aim is for the management committee, which meets every six weeks, to become representative of the ethnic minorities in the area.

A new trend in youth work, advocated by ILEA, is for minority groups to be more adequately catered for in youth clubs; and for, say 30 per cent of the work to be with girls. ILEA are also pushing strongly for positive discrimination, whereby less-suited committee members are elected onto the management committee in order to secure the appropriate racial balance for the area. It's praiseworthy to break down racism in that way, but it can result in mechanical management. It's management by recipe, and the minorities can actually feel *threatened* by being on the committee, because they're not used to functioning in that way. We also have a further difficulty, in that our management committee members obviously have to be Christians, but also members of our own church if they are to be elected onto a PCC sub-committee.

Our outpost on Kingsmead – known as Christ Church on the Mead – financially supports the youth project, to the tune of £10 per week. St Barnabas has given us several donations, the last one for £250. Though we get a sizeable grant from ILEA, we're always in need of extra funds just to maintain our current programme, let alone think about expansion. It would be nice if churches outside the borough – perhaps in well-to-do suburban areas – could support the work of churches like ours, in the inner-city. A number of churches in Barnet support the Homerton Space project, but St Paul's club receives no such support from outside the parish.

A recent development in our church life was for the parish to combine with nearby Risen Christ and All Souls, to form a team ministry. John Pearce had previously been priest-in-charge at All Souls, and the parishes had been working together informally as a team ministry for some time. With the official merger, John's curate at All Souls – Steve Cox, who's been there for nearly six years – became Team Vicar, while John became the first Team Rector. But John felt that the team needed new blood, and has now moved to a parish in West London. We're currently searching for a suitable replacement, who has the ability to hold the team together, while allowing the separate churches and projects to function in the way they always have. During the interregnum, the parish is in the hands of the Parish Wardens – one of whom is myself! I feel honoured that the parishioners have such trust and confidence in me.

If I have any regrets about the last few years, it's only that I've not kept more closely in touch with other churches and clubs in the area. Though I probably know most of the other Christian youth workers in East London, the only clubs that I'm really in contact with are the Good Shepherd at Bethnal Green – which runs its operations along very similar lines to ourselves – and St Mary's, Islington, which is the home church of my colleague Kevin Colman.

Most of the lively churches in the East End have programmes and emphases that are similar to those of our own parish which, incidentally, is now known as The Hackney Marsh Churches. For example, Brian Snelling, vicar of nearby St Luke's – a charismatic Anglican church in East London – in an article in *Today* magazine, explained the importance that his church gives to housegroups, in the growth and stability of the fellowship – an emphasis that my own church has followed since the sixties. "What can the Church do about the inner-city? It's got to be the Church. It's got to be the body of Christ," says Brian. "Sin, injustice, violence and crime happen everywhere, but it's thicker on the ground in the East End. The problem is with people, not structures. If the Gospel doesn't work in East London, then it doesn't work at all."

Just south of the river, Snowy, the youth worker at Cambridge University Mission, points out that the work of the Christian in the inner-city has to be done "on the street where you live". At one time there were more missions in Bermondsey than there were pubs. Because people were too ashamed to go to church in old clothes, many churches used to have facilities for poor people to borrow suits in which to attend church! It seems ludicrous now, but the principle is still a valid one. The deprived people of the inner-city still need to be given whatever it is that stops them from attending.

You find out a lot about a community by listening to its stories, and a church or club that keeps its ears open will soon discover what the particular problems are that keep people away from church. Usually, it's not clothes the people need; rather, it's a sense of the Church's irrelevance that stops them from attending. It's the local church that needs a new set of clothing – a new image – if it is to attract young urban-dwellers through its doors.

My contacts with a couple of secular clubs in the area supplement my own work in enabling me to keep my finger on the pulse. The senior worker at nearby Pedro Club is my ex-colleague, Peter Ellem, so there's naturally a lot of interaction between us. It's this kind of grassroots contact that makes one realise why events such as Mission to London are so irrelevant to young eastenders.

Mission to London, the 1984 evangelistic event centred on daily meetings at the Queen's Park Rangers stadium, was an embarrassment to me. It was in the wrong place, at the wrong time, for the wrong people. It may have been a useful event for suburban churches, but there was no way I was going to take a group of young people from Hackney across to the QPR stadium, because they wouldn't know how to act; they couldn't sit through a forty-five-minute talk. They can't even manage to listen to a two-minute discussion, so how were they going to let an evangelist they'd never heard of address them from the other side of a football stadium?

That sort of approach is just not going to work. There's an educational process needed before going over to one of those mass rallies, and the young eastenders haven't had it. What is needed is something local, something relevant to the people's needs, and something which communicates to them in a contemporary way.

Evangelists simply do not come to working-class inner-city areas and preach to us. They go to the white middle-classes instead. I remember going to a Christian drama production in Poplar and being amazed at the number of white middle-class people, and the almost total absence of black people. (In an area where perhaps

184

25 per cent of the population are black, I counted maybe three black faces in the audience of hundreds.) On another occasion Union Chapel, in the heart of working-class Islington, was used for a series of praise concerts. In spite of the location, virtually *no* local people came, and the place was full of Christians from the suburbs.

The recent *Faith in the City* report is another example of something well intentioned, but which ultimately leaves a lot to be desired. The report has attracted more attention than any other Church of England report for years, largely because of the unintentional publicity it received from central government.

It is actually an official report, with a lot of terminology and jargon. The demands which the report makes on the academic ability of the reader mean that the vast majority of people who live in deprived inner-city areas will be unable to *understand* what the report is saying about them and their environment. The report was intended largely for people outside Urban Priority Areas (UPAs), and all the recommendations are made either to the Church of England or to 'Government and Nation', not for urban-dwellers themselves. But this is the very root of the problem.

I said earlier that perhaps the most pressing inner-city problem is that of *powerlessness*. *Faith in the City* gives the knife another twist, by recommending a whole series of steps that could be taken to help out the urban-dweller. *It refuses to give back to the urban-dwellers any control over their own future.*

People who live in the inner-city are not *cases in need of help*. We have to accept that people in the inner-city have something positive – something beautiful – to give to society. People who have lived through poverty and adversity, have grown and developed as human beings, have insights of which the more pampered will never be aware. I believe that the true voice of the inner-city can be found echoed in the words of a member of another oppressed group – Australian aborigine Lilla Watson, who said: "If you have come to help me, you are wasting your time. But if you are here because your liberation is bound up with mine, then let us work together."

It's a poor sort of social change that is enforced from outside, by people who don't have to live with it if it goes wrong. It's surely better to give people in urban areas power over their own lives (as many of the report's recommendations on job creation would do) but then to let *them* decide what further action is needed.

For all the good intentions which become clearer once the excessive verbiage is pruned away, the report substantially ignores small-scale, local initiatives, by churches and individuals at grassroots level.

I know personally of many youth and community projects operating in East London, which seek to bring social change by changing the lives of individuals, through youth clubs, community centres, mums-and-toddlers groups, visiting the elderly, housing the homeless, addressing the problem of racism, helping drug addicts, and counselling those with family problems. In Spitalfields Crypt, a rehabilitation centre operates for alcoholics. In Canning Town, the Mayflower Centre is well-known for its influence on the local community. Only slightly less well-known is Lawrence Hall, in Newham.

I'm not suggesting that the report should have become bogged down with fine detail, but it is small-scale local projects such as these – not the major projects – which really bring about change. In the East End at least, if something isn't truly *local* (and by that, I mean not more than a couple of blocks away) then it isn't seen by local people as being relevant, or as having any impact on their lives.

I believe, from my experience in the East End, that the way to attract working-class people into church situations, where they can be presented with the Gospel, is through localised *social action* – showing that Jesus is really concerned with their work-a-day lives, and that Christians are too. We can do it through youth clubs, such as St Paul's, but we need also to be providing facilities for the elderly, the lonely, the sick, the unemployed, the ethnic minorities, and all the other factions with special needs.

The idea of Community Action as a means of building bridges and illustrating God's love is a key motif in many inner-city church projects. "It's clearly a front line responsibility," says Eddie Stride, the rector of Spitalfields. "If you're a Christian and love your neighbour, then you should try to improve his living conditions." To this end, Eddie feels, like myself, that it is essential that church helpers should live in the place of their ministry. He himself lives in a compact rectory in the shadow of the towering church which is a major landmark of the parish.

Alcoholics, dossers and tramps always seem to head for the East End where, though the streets are covered with garbage rather than paved with gold, a free meal can often be had, along with a bed for the night. Eddie's church specialises in taking in alcoholics to help them to 'dry out'. The crypt under the church has been converted to this end.

Working-class people need a lot of encouragement, and a lot of support if they are to become Christians and to remain strong in their faith; and not support for just a few weeks or months – but for perhaps *ten years*, till they are firmly rooted as Christians in their own community. But few Christians are prepared to offer that level of support, for such a long period. Too often, conversion causes people to come into so much greater a control of their lives, that they begin to prosper, and quickly move out into the suburbs. It's like trying to pastor on an elevator; we need people who are prepared to stay put.

A further problem caused by this exodus of new Christians is that leadership is constantly changing. "People, as they are converted and become better able to cope with life, often move out of the area," says our Team Vicar, Steve Cox, "We dearly need local people who feel it is right for them to stay. It's difficult for me to ask them to make that sacrifice." Along with other effective ministers in urban areas, Steve encourages lay people in the church to take a full part in the church's work. He believes, as I do, that East Londoners have immense ability, and that it is fully possible to have an every-member ministry in an area like Hackney. We trust people with responsibility, and look to the Lord to build his Church as he will. As Steve says: "God is making his own Church in the inner-city. It won't be a carbon copy of what it's like in other parts of the country."

If the first challenge is to the inner-city churches to use social action as a stepping stone to evangelism, then the second challenge must be directed towards the Christian in a suburban or rural situation. We know that you're praying for us, and we value that support; but is God asking you to do something more? There is a tremendous *need* for Christians to come to working-class urban areas, and to put down roots.

They are needed to go in and to encourage the working-class Christians – not from 'up front', but from 'behind the scenes'. They need to be willing to participate and to be part of a team. There's no place in urban ministry for the Super-Christian who wants to go it alone, or to go in and take control. The urban Church is full of gifted Christians who don't know how to use their gifts. Christians from outside are needed to come in, and to show us how to use the resources that we have, more effectively and efficiently.

To begin with, Christians outside the Urban Priority Areas (UPAs) need to educate themselves about the way life is for those less fortunate than themselves. It's really not good enough to sit in front of the TV and watch *East Enders*. (The *real* eastenders are every bit as interesting, but *their* problems don't end with the closing credits.) There's no real alternative to actually visiting a UPA (perhaps as a church group, visiting a UPA church) and experiencing a personal encounter with poverty, deprivation, powerlessness, unemployment, racism, crime, homelessness, and all those other ugly words. When the words are transformed into real experiences, then prayer for the UPAs can become focused; concern can become more real; and financial giving seems less onerous.

"The tide is coming in for the inner-city," John Pearce believes. "People want to find God, but we have to be where they are." John believes that, if the Church is to survive in such areas, it has to get alongside the people, to learn their culture and to identify with their needs.

The key thing is to start where people are, and to get to grips with their language. "In Hackney, people's vocabulary amounts to about five hundred words while the average vicar can command two thousand words," John explains. A minister has a lot of unlearning to do. Many of the immigrant population have an even smaller English vocabulary, and their traditions and culture are totally different from anything to which the average suburban-dweller has been used. An intensive re-learning exercise is essential for anyone who arrives fresh to the inner-city, with a view to ministry. Steve Cox realised that there could be no short cuts when he arrived straight from college: "The people, their culture and their problems vary from area to area. Hackney, for instance, is very diverse in itself."

We desperately need Christians to come and live in UPAs. With the escalating number of one-parent families, old people living alone, and unemployed young people; the breakdown in marriage; and poor housing conditions; Christians can offer love and security. They can show by their example that successful marriages *are* possible; they can open their homes and let young people see – perhaps for the first time – loving, caring parents. People pick up non-verbal communications as quickly as the spoken word; don't *say* you care, show them that you care. Put yourself out, by inviting the poor to Christmas and birthday parties. Open your heart.

There is great potential in the inner-city. If it is left to stagnate, then it will be lost forever. In the days before refrigeration, meat was kept from decay by rubbing salt into it. If the meat went bad, you couldn't blame the meat, only the lack of salt. We need more Christians to become the salt of the inner-city – to be enablers, and to teach by example. They need to have sticking power, and not run away at the weekends. People in urban areas have no escape, or release; they have to learn to cope with their situation where they are. If you really want to understand and to identify, then you have to *become* an inner-city dweller, and not a migratory bird that flies where the sun is.

We've had young people come to us from the suburbs for one year's work experience who have ended up staying for several years longer, because they felt that Hackney had become their home, and they didn't want to move. They stayed to learn, through the good and the bad. They learned empathy's real meaning – getting alongside means not just helping with the problem as it exists, but being willing to be involved with tomorrow's problems as well.

My prayer is that Christians in the suburbs will say "Break me, melt me, mould me, fill me – remake me. Let me follow your call, *not my job, or career.*" I believe that God wants people to come into the inner-city, to stay and belong, and to make it their home. They need to eat, drink and become; then they will belong. Many people are responding to the challenge. Please God, send us more!

16
YOUNG BLOOD IN THE CHURCH

The previous chapter was – if you like – part one of our conclusion, concerned with the needs of the Church in the city, and the social action needed to draw inner-city dwellers into the Church, where they can hear the Gospel. This final chapter is concerned with the needs that have to be satisfied once they are there, with particular reference to young people. We need to integrate the Church with the new generation. We shouldn't expect them to fit in with us. We need to fit in with them.

The third challenge then, is to the Church to pioneer radically-transformed modes of Christian worship. Though social action, stemming from a concern for justice, will draw the people of today into our churches, the problem is that Sunday worship in the average church is so old-fashioned and irrelevant that it will probably put off non-Christians from coming again!

"This isn't for us," they say. "We're not really interested in all these Victorian hymns; we like music that makes us move our feet. We don't need these dirges; we're not dead yet. Oh, and we can't understand what the lyrics are all about. What's this about 'there is a fountain filled with blood that's drawn from Immanuel's veins'? Bit ghoulish, isn't it, man? And this 'I lift my ebenezer' – cor blimey, it sounds like X-certificate stuff!"

Hymns which use agricultural references are a problem, too. It's all very well to sing "We plough the fields and scatter", but you won't see many fields being ploughed in Hackney. The imagery of a lot of hymns is totally at odds with urban (or even suburban) living.

Over at St Luke's, Brian Snelling says: "We're using fewer and fewer of the old hymns, because the language and imagery is so antiquated. Even I don't understand them, and I'm supposed to be trained!" *Mission Praise* is now the church's main music book – 'an inspired book' as Brian calls it. Guitars, piano, organ and tambourines are all used – and even a clarinet one Sunday – not simply to be modern, but also to draw out the skills and talents of people in the fellowship.

The churches in our team parish use a similar line-up of instruments for worship, with double bass and a wheezy accordion too. In the old days, when we ran regular youth services at St Paul's, I always used to sit-in on an old drum kit which the church had bought. It would be nice to have drums used again in our services.

Mission Praise is our regular music book – as it seems to be with most urban churches. It contains a few old hymns, but they're the loveliest ones. The choruses are our main musical fare, though it's a pity so many of them are lyrically a bit insubstantial. I feel that we need some pithy new lyrics to be written to some of the classic hymn tunes, or to modern pop tunes.

Down on Commercial Road, the only music to be heard is the squeal of brakes, the rumble of juggernauts butting their way towards Newham and, perhaps, the distant sounds of ship's hooters, out on the Thames. Noise pollution is matched by air pollution from the clouds of dust thrown up by the lorries; the grime seems to stick to your mouth, and the first thing you want to do when you arrive home is to clean your teeth, then shut the windows to keep out the noise. Yet, in a rectory not a stone's throw from all the hubbub, lives Chris Idle – who is best known for his work on the panel that compiled *Hymns for Today's Church*, and for his own hymns which have been published both in that collection and elsewhere. Chris though, is the rector of Limehouse and a man firmly committed to the work of the Church in the inner-city. As far as he's concerned, when it comes to music for use in worship in an urban church, variety is the keynote:

"Tunes that go with a lilt and which are easy to pick up usually go down well, but sometimes tunes that are easy to pick up are also easy to forget.

"There is a great enthusiasm for the new songs and choruses, and there's nothing wrong with having material which comes in for a month or so and then goes out again. But I think that it's good to learn some of the great old hymns, as long as we can understand the words.

"That's why I've been involved in revising the words of some of the great classics, to make them more comprehensible, and thus more usable."

Steve Cox heartily agrees with the continued use of some of the best of the old hymns, alongside the new. There are many West Indians at his church, who were brought up on the old hymns, and who enjoy the sense of security which comes from a more formal service, with some formal music. Not all the services are rigidly structured however; occasional evening services have an open pattern. "We have to cater both for those who want free worship and those who want a more ordered liturgy," says Steve. "There's security in structure. An open group can be more threatening."

Church music tends to cater for the people who listen to Radio 3 – with the occasional nod towards the Radio 2 listener. But the average urban-dweller today (and I don't just mean the young ones, either) is more in tune with Radio 1! Even updating the old hymns (as with *Hymns for Today's Church*) is little more than a holding operation – what we really need are the hymns for tomorrow's Church.

The keyboard instrument of today is not the organ or piano but the synthesiser; and unless you want your praise services to sound (to the un-Churched young person) like a requiem mass, you need a strong rhythm section behind the songs and hymns – and that means bass and drums.

If all that sounds very revolutionary, you need to remember that Wesley's hymns sounded revolutionary when they were first written. Charles Wesley was writing for a generation brought up on settings of the psalms, to specially-written church music. He turned tradition and convention to one side and wrote what in effect were the pop songs of his day, with well-known secular tunes. Even the organ was a revolutionary, new-fangled contraption when it was first introduced into worship. When William Booth founded The Salvation Army and had brass bands marching around Whitechapel, it was totally radical. Brass bands had previously been considered 'worldly'. Booth's actions were the equivalent, in today's terms, of using a soul band for worship.

But it isn't just church music that needs to become fresh and relevant (sing a *new* song to the Lord) the Bible readings and the sermon also need to be transformed. The 'Lessons' (and let's stop calling them that) need to be introduced with a few words that prepare the non-Christian for what is going to be read. We found with our Youth Services, that a dramatic reading, with several voices, was much more preferable to a 'straight' reading with one voice. But an 'enactment' – using a small drama group – is better still. Even if the reading doesn't lend itself to such treatment, it could be followed by a sketch to bring out the meaning. Most churches do these things only for special services. We believe that if the young generation is not to be lost forever, particularly in urban areas, drama has to become the norm for *most* services.

Now for the sermon. Sorry Vicar, but just getting up and talking for half an hour is not really on. It never was, to be quite honest. People remember 90 per cent of what they read, but *forget* 90 per cent of what they hear. They probably remembered more in the days of mass illiteracy, when most people learned everything by word of mouth. But today, young people and adults learn mostly from reading pictorial magazines, and from watching TV. Someone standing at the front talking is likely to be a sight they've not encountered since schooldays – and school is likely to bring back unpleasant memories for the semi-skilled urban dweller.

It's far better – we find – to talk for ten minutes at the most, and to try to use slides, video or an overhead projector to illustrate the talk (don't call it a sermon, that's an unpleasant word with a moralistic tone for many people.) Remember what I said back in chapter four, about how we always ensure that teaching comes in at more than one point in our Youth Service? Well, the same principle can profitably be applied to family worship, by introducing a short children's talk into the *early* part of the service and, possibly, by using an audio-visual presentation or a video. Scripture Union, Bible Society, BYFC (British Youth For Christ) and dozens of other Christian organisations produce suitable material, which will introduce a subject. In Freedom Gate, we often use clips from secular TV programmes or feature films; either when the 'message' is complementary or when it presents a standpoint which is commonly held, but which we want to refute.

A word about lighting. If you went to a concert, or to the theatre, and the house lights were on for the whole show, it would probably spoil your evening. Lighting is intended to draw your attention towards what is important, and away from what is irrelevant. But during a church service, the main lighting is always on throughout, illuminating a whole range of visual distractions to draw people's attention away from the service itself. Is is really any wonder that young people often become restless, or find it difficult to follow what is going on? Of course, the lights need to be turned up over the congregation during the hymns so people can read the words, but to have the whole interior illuminated during the talk is a pure distraction.

Other pointers to successful services that relate to the people of today are: talks need to be relevant to people's needs; the language needs to be the language of the people; some inner-city churches have found it helpful for the congregation to be able to give feedback after the talk, with questions and comments; other churches use open-air witness to attract people along to their outreach meetings.

Of course, a lot of a church's work goes on in mid-week meetings; but eventually, a new or potential convert is going to come up against a Sunday service and – if it's irrelevant to his/her needs and/or culture – all the good work can easily be undone.

I've talked about our Youth Bible Studies and Home Groups, here at the Hackney Marsh Churches, in great detail in chapter four. But perhaps I can add to that here, with some comments made by other ministers in the area, when they were asked what really works in the inner-city. Anything that creates a centre of belonging and gives people the feeling that they are somebody, that they count; Home Groups are taking off in a very positive way; being real about relationships; being able to help non-Christians with their problems without trying to over-spiritualise; and sharing meals together, either after Sunday worship every couple of months, or special evening outreach meals usually tied in with church festivals.

Young people desperately need to feel *secure*. That's one reason why church services, and not just special youth services, need to be orientated towards making them feel at home; and also why the special needs of young people need to be catered for in special mid-week meetings. There are a number of steps that youth leaders, pastors and parents can take to help individually. These include: taking time to listen and talk to the youngsters without criticising, accusing or threatening; showing affection regularly (parents can hug or cuddle their children, whereas a youth leader – unless he/she is going to risk accusations of being gay or 'on the make' – can only put an arm around a young person's shoulder); allowing them the freedom to express their own personalities, without trying to make them conform; helping them to develop interests in healthy activities such as sports, arts or entertainments; giving them a good example by not smoking, over-indulging in drink, or over-emphasising sex at the expense of love and affection; and above all, simply being available to talk, share and counsel.

Of course, many churches – particularly the house churches – already do all this, and have probably read the last few pages with great amusement. But others will have the more serious problem of wanting to follow the pattern I've outlined (in part at least) but are worried about how the older members will react. It may prove necessary to introduce newer forms of service alongside the old for a while, while the older members learn to adapt. But the problem of living with change can be a thorny one. When Ray Bakke, an expert on urban mission, came to London in September 1985, he tackled this whole issue in some detail:

"The seven last words spoken by any church are, *'We never did it that way before!'* Changing 'survivors' into achievers is the first step towards change. Before setting goals and aiming at the future, you have to recreate their memories, by asking questions like: *How did you become a Christian? How long have you been in this church?* and *What has excited you the most down the years?* and *If you could bring about changes in the church, what would you like to happen?* Spend about three hours discussing these questions with each of the older members of the church. Most of them will *reminisce* about the sort of thing you want to do now! Incorporate their stories into your talks. Tell them what they did and what their parents did. This gives not only permission, but a mandate to change. Get them to tell appropriate stories about changes that happened in the past, *during services* – 'The view from the pew.' This is exactly what the Old Testament prophets did, with their constant reference back to Jewish history – 'Do you remember when you were in the wilderness…'"

Bakke also had something to say about what congregations can do with old pastors who are reluctant to change: "They're like Henry Ford, the motor car manufacturer. He wouldn't change, even when research showed that people wanted motor cars in colours other than black.

"Offer to take the pastor to see how other churches operate. Ask him the three basic questions above; particularly about what has excited him the most down the years, and what he would like to see the church doing in future."

Ray feels that one of the first things that must be done if a church is to be truly effective in its task of winning people for God, is to create a mission model that the congregation are happy with. We need to look at how a church and its mission relate:

"Most of the barriers to effective mission are 'internal' to the church, i.e. distrust.

"Churches often feel *threatened* by competition (from other religions, denominations, etc.) In Manila, for example, there are so many churches that the population have become religious consumers.

"A city is a *conflict* environment, but most pastors don't know how to live in such an environment. (i.e. If a stripper becomes a Christian and gives up her occupation, what does she do instead?) In 1980, there was *no* urban preparation for candidates by *any* missionary agency, even though most missionaries came from rural areas. In consequence, missionaries felt thwarted in an urban environment.

"We need to take a fresh look at missionary work to unreached peoples! There are now more unreached peoples living in large cities than in geographically distant areas. For example, if you want to reach Jews, go to New York, because there are more Jews there than in the whole state of Israel; 14 per cent of Parisians are from Algeria; there are a lot of Japanese people in Brazil; there are fifty thousand Yugoslavians living in Stockholm; and Chicago is the second largest Polish city in the world!"

Neater to home, we're rapidly reaching the point where there are more West Indian people in the inner-city areas of our own country than there are in the West

Indies! It's no longer necessary to go abroad in order to be a missionary to other races. Ray has a few tips on how to evangelise them, too:

"Visit men at their place of work whenever possible, because that is when they are 'themselves'. They think of themselves as being 'a lawyer', 'an electrician' or whatever.

"We need to create a sense of beauty in the inner-city. We need to break down barriers between the Church and the community. One way to overcome alienation is through community contact by '*networking*'. This consists of new people contacting members of the local community and saying, 'I'm new. I need help.' (That's usually a good way to get them on your side!) Ask them 'Can you tell me the most important lessons you've learned in your time here?'"

Ray made a point of giving over one day per week to make these contacts, whenever he moved to a new church. As a result of this, he discovered that the local police responded to a large number of calls relating to domestic violence. The church was able to take on some of the police's job in handling these incidents. But the church has had to earn the right to get involved, through its interest in the neighbourhood.

"Different churches don't really get together enough. (There's an old saying that 'When the tide goes out, each shrimp has its own puddle!') Outsiders perceive this, and use it as an excuse to avoid Christianity. Different churches need to meet together more often, and have greater contact with each other.

"After visiting other churches, a new pastor or church worker should visit social agencies; too many people don't approach social agencies until an emergency occurs. Perhaps a church could even instigate the formation of a *forum*, comprising of key people from churches, local industry, social agencies, politics, etc., so that people in different professions can interrelate and act together on mutually relevant topics.

"*Within* a church, pastors and church youth workers

should take someone else with them to every call they make, so that an extra person can discover how to do the pastoral tasks!"

Young people have the wrong idea of what the Church is; they think it's an outdated, old-fashioned hang-over from the past. For an African, or an Asian, it has to be relevant to *their* history and culture. The old ways of church worship have no relevance to contemporary culture. Churches need to do what we at the Hackney Marsh Churches have to do; to look at where they're at, realise what they're trying to do, and decide where they need to change. If a percentage of the congregation *can't* change, then perhaps it's right for them to move on; but using some of Ray Bakke's tips may make that unnecessary.

I sometimes think that the Church of England is still in the sixteenth century, and fails to relate to twentieth-century people. Our responsibility is to the Church of tomorrow. They're depending on us to hand them on a truly relevant Church. If we get it wrong and give them a sixteenth-century Church, what chance have they got? It's got to start with us, because we're responsible. We've got to start changing and becoming relevant to today.

It's not just the Anglican Church though. Alan Walmsley, in his summary of the United Reformed Church's *Report of the work of the Church among the Young* says:

> The separation of the work among young people from the work of the adult church is a defect of prime importance . . . It falls short of the wide community life and warmth of personal relationships we should expect to find in a church.

Walmsley refers to the necessity for fundamental changes such as

> ending the Sunday School as a separate organisation, the

termination of the usual form of Sunday morning service with fixed liturgy, set lessons and sermon, and changes in the organisations of mid-week activities and in the use of the church and other buildings... There is the alternative of starting another morning service on a church community basis.

Space prevents me from discussing the other denominations. But basically, we all need to remember that there is no fixed or final form of Christian faith. The Church's task is to explore and seek to discover the truth for today. We need to see the Church as a community for Christian education, mission and social change.

In the words of David Watson: "Evangelism and social action are the two blades of a pair of scissors; if we have one without the other, we lose our cutting edge." The Church's mission is *more* than just saving people's souls. Salvation means saving people from poverty and injustice, too. You only have to read Exodus to realise that when the Israelites were freed from captivity in Egypt – the great liberation which the New Testament writers see as foreshadowing the salvation that Christ was to bring – there was fundamentally a *social, political* and *cultural* liberation, and only secondarily a spiritual liberation. We have to free people from poverty, powerlessness and injustice as well as from their slavery to sin. We've got to stop being so heavenly-minded that we're no earthly good.

We have to ensure that our church structures and traditions don't impose fresh injustice and powerlessness on our converts. (That means ensuring that vital decisions affecting church life are notified to the membership, and ensuring that PCC agendas and minutes (or their equivalents in the nonconformist churches) are posted where they can be read by *all* the church membership!)

It's the same as with youth work. We've got to be persistent and what we're offering has got to be *relevant*. If it isn't it will be bypassed. If it's archaic and out of date, it will not be used.

201

In this book, we've tried to communicate how a church and youth project can be effective, specifically with inner-city youngsters, though the lessons are mostly appropriate to *any* youth situation. The first half looked at what it is like to be a youth worker in the inner-city, while the second half dealt with the major issues that I'm constantly faced with in my day-to-day work, and related the specific problems to the ministry of the Christian Church in general.

These issues are essential topics for any urban youth-club programme, because they are issues relevant to the young people's everyday lives. They may, at present, be less relevant to many rural and suburban clubs but – with the increasing urbanisation of society – it's only a matter of time before the problems of the inner-city filter out into provincial towns and suburban commuter belts.

If the Church takes young people seriously, then the young people will take the Church seriously. We must aim to be relevant; and in doing so, we must make *change* our friend – not our enemy.

Young people today have become like troops on a battlefield, without even being given the opportunity to learn that there is a war going on. But, make no mistake, there *is* a conflict raging around young people. It is a spiritual war against the dehumanising effects of city life that make the good news of Jesus seem like an impossible dream.

It is up to the Church to make itself more relevant, in order to stem the wastage of human life, and to dam the tide of souls being carried off to a lost eternity without Jesus. I am privileged to be on the front line in the Church's fight.

Bibliography

This listing is not exhaustive. It excludes books which are over-technical, which are difficult to obtain, or which substantially duplicate other books already listed. No books published later than 1985 have been listed. Books have been classified according to the area of urban youth work for which they are the most useful, though obviously many books are useful in several different areas. Exceptionally useful books are marked with an asterisk.

Young People in Urban Areas (Wastage)

Birnie, I.H., *Christianity and Youth* (Edward Arnold: 1978)
Eastman, M., (Ed) *Making Known the Good News* (1980)
*Harrison, P., *Inside the Inner City* (Pelican: 1982)
Lennon, D., *Young World!* (Overseas Missionary Fellowship Books: 1979)
Murphy, J., and Fearon, M, *Devil's Island* (Marshall-Pickering: 1985)

Young People and Youth Clubs (A Day at a Time)

Kennedy, A., *Shadows of Adolescence* (National Youth Bureau: 1984)
Neale, E., *Go Down in the City* (Scripture Union: 1974)

Open Youth Work

Andrew, C., *A Handbook of Parish Youth Work* (Church Information Office: 1984)
Brake, M., *The Sociology of Youth Culture and Youth Subcultures* (Routledge and Kegan Paul: 1980)
Eggleston, J., *Adolescence and Community* (Edward Arnold: 1976)
*Wilson, P., *Gutter Feelings* (Marshall-Pickering: 1985)

Youth Evangelism

General Synod Board Of Education, *A Kind of Believing* (Church Information Office: 1977)

General Synod Board Of Education, *Bewildered but Believing* (Church Information Office: 1978)

Halls, D., *Using the Bible with Youth* (Bible Society: 1981)

Little, P., *How to Give Away Your Faith* (Inter Varsity Press: 1966)

Milson, F., *Youth in the Local Church* (1981)

Wilkerson, D., *The Cross and the Switchblade* (Lakeland: 1962)

Training

Chelms, S., *Creative Training* (National Association of Youth Clubs [NAYC]: 1981)

*Coleman, L., *Six Training Sessions* (Scripture Union: 1983)

Eastman, M., (Ed) *Inside Out* (Falcon: 1976)

Redman, W., *Help! Finding and Keeping Volunteers for the Youth Club* (National Association of Youth Clubs [NAYC]: 1981)

Taylor, P., *Just Something to Do* (National Youth Bureau (NYB]: 1984)

Detached Youth Work

Edginton, J., *Avenues Unlimited* (National Youth Bureau: [NYB] 1979)

Robins, D., *Knuckle Sandwich* (Pelican: 1978)

The Pressures

*Redman, W., *Guidelines to Finding Your Own Support* (NAYC: 1981)

Youth Development Trust (YDT), *Reflected Images* (Youth Development Trust [YDT]: 1983)

Programmes and Expansion

*Bennet (et al), *No Kidding!* (National Association of Youth Clubs [NAYC]: 1983)

Dowmunt, T., *Video with Young People* (Inter-Action Inprint sic: 1980)

Sutherland, A., *Life Puzzle* (Jonquil Publishing: 1984)

Education

Cockram, L., *Rehearsing to be Adults* (National Youth Bureau [NYB]: 1978)

*Gowar, M., *Starting Out* (Collins Educational: 1984)

Hudson, K., *The Language of the Teenage Revolution* (Macmillan: 1983)

National Council For Volunteer Youth Services (NCVYS), *Young People and Decisions* (NCVYS: 1981)

O'Donnell, G., *Communication Skills* (Careers Research and Advisory Centre: 1984)

Home Life

Cashmore, E.E., *No Future* (Heinemann: 1984)

Claerbaut, D., *Urban Ministry* (Zondervan: 1983)

Office Of Population Census And Surveys, *1981 Census Statistics* (HMSO: 1982)

Roberts, K., *Youth and Leisure* (George Allen and Unwin: 1983)

Whittaker, D., *Youth in Society* (Longman: 1984)

Homelessness

Brandon, *The Survivors* (Routledge and Kegan Paul: 1980)

Common Agricultural Policy (CAP), *Beyond the Hostel* (CAP: 1982)

Drake, M., *Single and Homeless* (HMSO: 1981)

GMYA/NAYC, *Homelessness Project Annual Report* (Greater Manchester Youth Association [GMYA] National Association of Youth Clubs [NAYC]: 1982)

*GMYA/NAYC, *Homelessness Project Training Pack* (GMYA/NAYC: 1980)

Unemployment

Casson, M., *Youth Unemployment* (Careers Research and Advisory Centre: 1979)

Hirsch, D., *Youth Unemployment – A Background Paper* (Macmillan: 1983)

Jackson, M., *Youth Unemployment* (Youth Aid: 1985)

Sandon, A., *Unemployment and YOP in the Inner City* (Youth Aid: 1982)

Violence

Wyndham Place Trust, *Violence in Britain* (WPT: 1980)

Crime

Baldwin, J., *Give 'Em a Break* (National Youth Bureau: 1982)

National Youth Bureau, *Young People and the Police* (National Youth Bureau [NYB]: 1979)

Rae, M., *First Rights* (National Council for Civil Liberties: 1981)

Racism

*Cashmore, et al (Eds), *Black Youth in Crisis* (George Allen and Unwin: 1982)

Commission for Racial Equality, *Ethnic Minority & Youth Unemployment* (CRE: 1980)

Day, M. and Marshal, D. (Eds), *Black Kids, White Kids, What Hope?* (1978)

Scarman, Lord., *The Scarman Report* (Penguin: 1982)

Drink

Caruana, S., *Teaching about Alcohol and Drinking* (1978)

*Judith, S., *How to Cope with an Alcoholic Parent* (Canongate: 1979)

Kessel, N., and Walton, H., *Alcoholism* (Pelican: 1965)

Moses, D., *Are You Driving Our Children to Drink?* (Van Nostrand: 1975)

Drugs

Beschnen, (Ed) *Youth Drug Abuse* (Lexington Books: 1979)

O'Connor, D., *Glue Sniffing and Volatile Substance Abuse* (Gower: 1984)

Ralls, M.T., *Escape to Reality* (Marshall–Pickering: 1985)

Sex

Champlin, J., *Don't You Really Love Me?* (Ave Maria Press: 1976)

*Dominian, J., *The Growth of Love and Sex* (Darton, Longman and Todd: 1982)

Prince, J., *God Thought of Sex First* (Scripture Union: 1978)

Urban Mission (Church in the City)

*Cave, D., *Jesus is Your Best Mate* (Marshall-Pickering: 1985)

Christian Action, *Faith in the City – A Call for Action by Church and Nation* (Christian Action: 1985)